THE ART OF ADVOCACY IN ADMINISTRATIVE LAW AND PRACTICE

THE ART OF ADVOCACY IN ADMINISTRATIVE LAW AND PRACTICE

BY LISA MILLER

AMERICAN**BAR**ASSOCIATION

Solo, Small Firm and
General Practice Division

Cover design by Kelly Book/ABA Design

Printed in the United States of America.

23 22 21 20 19   5 4 3 2 1

ISBN: 978-1-64105-237-5
e-ISBN: 978-1-64105-238-2

Library of Congress Cataloging-in-Publication Data

Names: Miller, Lisa L., author. | American Bar Association. Solo, Small Firm and
General Practice Division, sponsoring body.
Title: The art of advocacy in administrative law and practice / Lisa L. Miller.
Description: First. | Chicago : American Bar Association, 2019. | Includes index. | Summary:
"The content of this volume is focused on the Administrative Procedures Acts (APAs)
of the U.S. federal government (the busiest administrative forum), along with California,
Texas, Florida, New York, and Illinois, the largest states with well-developed administrative
environments. The general discussions in this volume can help guide practitioners as
they follow the APA requirements of the U.S. federal government, a particular state, or a
territory of the United States in which counsel's matter is in process"—Provided by publisher.
Identifiers: LCCN 2019024627 (print) | LCCN 2019024628 (ebook) | ISBN
9781641052375 (paperback) | ISBN 9781641052382 (ebook)
Subjects: LCSH: Administrative law—United States.
Classification: LCC KF5402.M55 2019 (print) | LCC KF5402 (ebook) |
DDC 342.73/06—dc23
LC record available at https://lccn.loc.gov/2019024627
LC ebook record available at https://lccn.loc.gov/2019024628

Discounts are available for books ordered in bulk. Special consideration is given to state bars, CLE programs, and other bar-related organizations. Inquire at Book Publishing, ABA Publishing, American Bar Association, 321 N. Clark Street, Chicago, Illinois 60654-7598.

www.shopABA.org

Contents

Preface

The U.S. federal government, as well as every state and territory of the United States, maintains an expansive administrative apparatus that each year affects millions of individuals, businesses, and institutions. Though they have much in common, the federal government, each state government, and the government of every U.S. territory have each developed unique approaches to administrative law and process.

For this reason, we have focused the content of this volume on the Administrative Procedures Acts (APAs) of the U.S. federal government (the busiest administrative forum), along with California, Texas, Florida, New York, and Illinois, the largest states with well-developed administrative environments. The particular requirements of the APAs for these states and the federal government demonstrate generally how administrative law and advocacy function, and highlight how they variously approach administrative law and process. In addition, we have included as many examples of commonly occurring legal challenges as reasonably possible, culled from all other U.S. states and territories.

The general discussions in this volume can help guide practitioners as they follow the APA requirements of the U.S. federal government, a particular state, or a territory of the United States in which counsel's matter is in process. Because the federal government, every state, and every territory has a body of law to guide participants in the administrative process, advocates should consult these governmental resources for guidance and direction in their particular locations. Practitioners should use the examples in this volume as illustrative instructional guidance.

Overview of Administrative Law

Administrative Law: The Basics

Administrative law is all the rules created by administrative agencies and government departments.[1] Administrative law is so ubiquitous and widespread that even clients with traditional civil law cases frequently face related administrative actions.[2] In addition, the number of professions subject to administrative licensure is rapidly expanding. As a result, well-rounded counsel can serve new and existing clients well by understanding the reach of the administrative state and mastering administrative law and practice.

State legislatures and Congress pass laws; agencies implement these laws as part of administrative law. Administrative law governs the creation and operation of the government's administrative agencies. Most regulations, and the decisions

---

1. The body of administrative law in the United States can be, and sometimes is, affected by civil law appeals of administrative law–centered matters. Fairly recent examples of this are *Lippman v. City of Oakland*, __ Cal. 5th __ (2018) (appeal of an administrative law code enforcement decision by the City of Oakland); and *Rasooly v. City of Oakley* (2018) __ Cal. App. 5th ___ (A152709; in the Court of Appeal of the State of California, 1st Appellate District) (Contra Costa County Super. Ct. No. N16-1492) (filed Oct. 25, 2018; publication ordered Nov. 21, 2018). The municipal code ordinance's plain language requires that notice of code violation be served by personal service, certified mail, or by affixing a copy to the structure. This establishes a hierarchy of acceptable means of providing notice. Any one of these means is "service." As a result, the ordinance's "nail & mail" procedures are not constitutionally deficient (even absent efforts at personal service).

2. For example, litigation over real property–related issues can trigger a visit from the local municipal code enforcement officer, possibly resulting in an administrative agency citation being issued. Once the client decides to fight the action and fees demanded in the citation, counsel will need to advise and guide the client through the administrative law and litigation process. A similar analysis results when a licensed professional (such as a public school teacher or a registered nurse) is cited for driving under the influence; the state likely will initiate a negative action on the client's professional license. Counsel who understand the expansion of the administrative state as it branches off the client's existing legal conflict are ahead of the curve in excellent client service and law firm business development. This volume provides a structure against which counsel can build an administrative case for clients facing administrative actions, either in tandem with an existing legal matter or completely independent of any other legal representation.

that result from their application and enforcement, flow from state, territory, and federal administrative agencies. This is the confluence of civil enforcement activity and administrative law practice.

Administrative Agencies

Administrative agencies support orderly government. When legislatures pass laws on complicated issues, they need help figuring out the granular aspects of implementation and enforcement of these laws. This triggers administrative agencies (and similar government departments) to develop all the particulars for implementation and enforcement of these new laws.[3] To do this, agencies write and enact rules and regulations. Uncertainty sometimes arises regarding the powers granted to administrative agencies, the substantive rules these agencies make, and the legal relationships among agencies, government bodies, and the public. All of these are areas for counsel to argue when representing clients on the receiving end of administrative enforcement actions.

Federal administrative agencies are generally created by Congress and the president; they have the power to create agencies and delegate defined powers.[4] The president creates "executive" agencies; Congress creates "independent" agencies.[5]

Examples of Administrative Agencies

Federal Administrative Agencies
Well-known federal administrative agencies include the following:
- Food and Drug Administration
- Department of Justice
- Internal Revenue Service
- Securities and Exchange Commission

State Administrative Agencies
Some interesting state administrative agencies follow:[6]

---

3. Agencies can also be called boards, departments, divisions, commissions, or similar titles.
4. For example, in a unanimous decision regarding the powers of the Federal Trade Commission, the Supreme Court held, to the extent that the agency exercises any executive function, it does so in the discharge and effectuation of its quasi-legislative or quasi-judicial powers or as an agency of the legislative or judicial departments of the government (*Humphrey's Executor v. United States*, 295 U.S. 602 (1935)). Without this recognition, the existence of administrative agencies would be unconstitutional, because agencies exercise several types of powers, including law-making and sanction-leveling.
5. The major difference between executive agencies and independent agencies is that the president may not remove the head of an independent agency without "just cause." Heads of executive agencies serve at the will of the president; they can be removed at any time.
6. California agencies are listed online at http://www.ca.gov/Agencies. Texas state agencies are listed at https://www.tsl.texas.gov/apps/lrs/agencies/index.html. Florida administrative agencies are at https://dos.myflorida.com/library-archives/research/florida-information/government/state-resources/state-agency-homepages. Administrative agencies for New York state are at https://www.ny.gov/agencies#all-agencies, for example.

California

- Boating and Waterways Commission
- Bureau of Firearms
- Horse Racing Board
- Lottery Commission

Texas

- Anatomical Board
- Feed and Fertilizer Control Service (Office of the State Chemist)
- Commission on Jail Standards

Florida

- Department of Citrus
- Florida Geological Survey
- Agency for State Technology

New York

- Office of Counter Terrorism
- Office of Medicaid Inspector General
- Thruway Authority

Illinois

- Budgeting for Results Commission
- Executive Ethics Commission
- State Fair

State governments encompass administrative agencies that implement, execute, and enforce laws passed by state legislatures. State agencies are generally created in the same manner as federal agencies and frequently mimic major federal agencies (for example, California and Federal Department of Justice, California and Federal Department of the Treasury, Texas and Federal Department of Agriculture).

State residents often deal with administrative agencies and administrative law when they seek benefits in a state.[7] Administrative law broadly protects public interests, not private rights, and agencies must act within constitutional parameters (always!).

---

7. For example, California has CalFresh, formerly Food Stamps; CalWORKs (a welfare program that gives cash aid and services); Head Start (implementing the Federal Head Start program); Low Income Home Energy Assistance Program (LIHEAP) Block Grant, funded by the Federal Department of Health and Human Services; Medicaid/Medi-Cal, California's Medicaid health care program; California National School Breakfast and Lunch Program (the U.S. Department of Agriculture funds school meal and milk programs); Special Milk Program, a federally funded program helping schools provide milk to children; Special Supplemental Nutrition Program for Women, Infants, and Children (WIC), which provides supplemental foods and nutrition education.

> ### Example
>
> California's Division of Occupational Safety and Health, known as Cal/OSHA, protects workers' health and safety, as well as passengers riding elevators, amusement rides, and tramways.
> Cal/OSHA's administrative activities include the following:
> * Setting standards and enforcing them
> * Providing outreach and education
> * Issuing permits, licenses, certifications, registrations, and approvals

U.S. Federal Administrative Law

Limits and directives on actions by federal agencies are based in the federal Administrative Procedure Act (the FAPA).[8] The FAPA governs internal procedures of federal administrative agencies, including how they interact with the public. The FAPA prohibits improper agency behavior. In addition to addressing agency rule making, adjudication, and licensure,[9] the FAPA contemplates an elastic definition of "agency."[10] The FAPA includes both the Freedom of Information Act (FOIA[11]) and the Privacy Act.[12]

Turning to state Administrative Procedure acts generally, three populous states illustrate how several Administrative Procedures Acts, enacted by different states, function: California, Texas, and Florida, as follows:

* California agencies are included in both the California Administrative Procedure Act (Cal.-APA) and the California Office of Administrative Law (OAL) Regulations.[13] Cal.-APA establishes rulemaking procedures and standards for California's state agencies. California regulations must also be adopted in compliance with standards adopted by the OAL.[14]

---

8. The federal Administrative Procedure Act is codified at 5 U.S.C. §§ 551-559 (2012).

9. Licensure is defined as: "The granting of licenses, especially to practice a profession; the granting of permission, generally by a government agency, allowing an organization or individual to engage in a practice or activity, which, without the license, would be illegal." For more information, visit https://www.merriam-webster.com/dictionary/licensure.

10. "agency" means each authority of the government of the United States, whether or not it is within or subject to review by another agency (it does not include the U.S. Congress, U.S. courts, the governments of U.S. territories or possessions, the government of the District of Columbia; or, except as to the requirements of section 552 of this title. . . . 5 U.S.C. § 552, FAPA § 3).

11. The federal Freedom of Information Act is codified at 5 U.S.C. § 552 (2012) (advocates should check for pocket part supplements before citing).

12. The federal Privacy Act is codified at 5 U.S.C. § 552a (2012).

13. California Office of Administrative Law, *Administrative Procedure Act & OAL Regulations*, www.ola.gov.ca; https://oal.ca.gov/publications/administrative_procedure_act (last visited September 25, 2017).

14. See California Code of Regulations, Title 1, § 1-280.

- The Texas Government Code, Administrative Procedure and Practice, covers state administrative law and practice in the Lone Star state.[15]
- The Florida Administrative Procedure Act is found in Title 10, Part X, Chapter 120 of the Florida Statutes.[16]

All U.S. states and territories have enacted or adopted APAs, many of which generally track the FAPA.[17] The FAPA procedures give the public an opportunity to participate in the adoption of federal regulations. It ensures that regulations are clear, necessary, and legally sound.

---

15. Title 10, General Government, Subtitle A: Chapter 2001: Administrative Procedure.
16. Found online at: http://www.leg.state.fl.us/Statutes/index.cfm?App_mode=Display_Statute& URL=0100-0199/0120/0120.html.
17. The Administrative Procedure Act statutes for the top 10 U.S. states (by population) follow: New York (New York Consolidated Laws, Sec. 202, State Administrative Procedure Act (SAPA)); Florida (Chapter 120, Florida Statutes, the Administrative Procedure Act (FAPA)); Illinois (Illinois Compiled Statutes, General Provisions, 5 ILCS 100/, Illinois Administrative Procedure Act); Pennsylvania (Pennsylvania Annotated Statutes, Title 2, Administrative Law and Procedure, Chapters 1, 5, and 7); Ohio (Ohio Revised Code, Chapter 119: Administrative Procedure); Georgia (Georgia Administrative Procedure Act, Official Code of Georgia Annotated, Title 50, Chapter 13, Article 1); Michigan (Michigan Compiled Laws, Act 306 of 1969, Administrative Procedures Act of 1969 (Act 306, The APA)); North Carolina (North Carolina Administrative Procedure Act, Chapter 150B, General Statutes of North Carolina (APA)); New Jersey (Administrative Procedure Act, N.J.S.A. 52:14B-1, *et seq.*).

2

Purposes and Principles of Administrative Law

Administrative law revolves around three basic principles:

- Safeguarding the rights and interests of individuals
- Holding government officials accountable regarding, among other things, their exercise of government power
- Ensuring that administrative decisions and actions are rational, fair, consistent, and transparent, to ensure reasonably consistent interpretation of regulatory law and consistent enforcement of regulations

Administrative law has three basic purposes:

- Restraining government abuse of power and enforcing government accountability
- Fostering impartial decision making and protecting members of the public from infringement of their rights
- Supporting the rule of law and good public administration

Role of the Federal Administrative Procedure Act

The FAPA restrains improper federal agency behavior, protects public safety, and secures entitlements (unemployment benefits, for example). It addresses three agency functions: rulemaking, adjudication, and licensure.

What Is a Rule?

Rules are implementations, interpretations, or prescriptions related to law or policy. Rules describe agency organization, procedures, or practices, and include approval of, or prescription for, future rates, wages, and related concepts or practices bearing on these.[1]

Adjudication (Agency Enforcement)

Agency adjudication can be either formal or informal. Formal adjudication is required by explicit statutory language and contemplates notice of the opportunity for a hearing and creation of an official record of the hearing proceedings. An administrative judge presides over the hearing. The judge renders a decision, which can be considered final or which can be appealed up the agency's chain of command (usually only final agency decisions are eligible for judicial review in a civil court).

Hearing procedures are set by each agency and are subject to the requirements of constitutional due process if

- the hearing involves issues of adjudicative facts,[2] or facts that affect a small, individualized group; and
- the hearing involves the possibility of a deprivation of a property or a liberty interest.[3]

Licensure

When a professional license (cosmetology and barbering, podiatrists, and hundreds more) is required by law, agencies must adhere to the formal rule-making and adjudication requirements in the relevant federal or state APA (other license applications are governed entirely by internal agency rules).[4]

Judicial Review

Final agency decisions are subject to review in the courts, which decide questions of law, interpret constitutional and statutory provisions, and determine the meaning or applicability of terms in agency actions. Judicial review in the courts

---

1. The FAPA sets out specific rule-making guidance agencies must use: they must give notice of proposed rule making (published in the Federal Register), as well as giving the legal authority allowing the agency to propose the new rule (and its contents). Once the agency provides public notice of the proposed new rule, it must solicit and accept public comment and consider it. Occasionally, agencies must hold traditional hearings as part of formal rule making; their decisions must be based on evidence provided in the hearing record.

2. Adjudicative fact is a fact that is either legally operative or "even so important as to be controlling on some question of law." Adjudicative facts are those "which concern the parties to some dispute and are helpful in determining the proper outcome in the case" (Cornell Law School, *Adjudicative Fact*, www.law.cornell.edu; https://www.law.cornell.edu/wex/adjudicative_fact (last visited September 25, 2017).

3. *Board of Regents of State Colleges v. Roth*, 408 U.S. 564 (1972).

4. A more complete discussion of administrative law and practice regarding professional licensure can be found in this volume at p. 117.

is based on the record developed by the agency. Reviewing courts may require agencies to take action that was unlawfully withheld or unreasonably delayed. They may find unlawful and set aside agency action, findings, and conclusions that are any of the following:

- Arbitrary, capricious, an abuse of discretion, or otherwise not in accordance with law
- Contrary to constitutional right, power, privilege, or immunity
- In excess of statutory jurisdiction, authority, or limitations, or short of statutory right
- Without observance of procedure required by law
- Unsupported by substantial evidence (in cases subject to §§ 556, 557 of Title 5 (Government Organization and Employees) of the U.S. Code) or otherwise reviewed on the record of an agency hearing provided by statute or
- Unwarranted by the facts (to the extent that the facts are subject to trial *de novo* by the reviewing court)

State Administrative Procedures Acts: Overviews and Examples

California Administrative Procedure Act

The California Administrative Procedure Act (Cal.-APA) Cal.-APA ensures uniformity and openness in the procedures used by California agencies.[5] The Cal.-APA has broad authority covering regulations, rule-making procedures, and adjudications. It is the public's conduit to participation in the formation of state regulation Cal.-APA.[6] Its purpose is to ensure clear, necessary, and legally valid regulations. Generally, anyone (or any group) can request California agencies to change, adopt, or repeal regulations. Agencies are limited in the process, however, by the scope of authority in the statute that created the agency (enabling statute) and applicable law.

The Cal.-APA created the Office of Administrative Law (OAL). The OAL reviews proposed California state agencies' administrative regulations for compliance with the Cal.-APA, sends regulations to the California secretary of state, and publishes regulations in the California Code of Regulations.

Note
The Cal.-APA was adopted almost one year before the FAPA. The FAPA largely traces the Cal.-APA.

---

5. The FAPA is the major source for federal administrative agency law.
6. Cal. Gov't. Code §§ 11340-11365.

Texas Administrative Procedure Act

The Texas Administrative Procedure Act (Tex.-APA)[7] covers in detail administrative adjudication, government rule making, the process of judicial review for various types of agency action, and enforcement of agency orders and rules. The Tex.-APA outlines general legal requirements to which state agencies must conform when they adopt regulations or hold hearings for contested citation (or other enforcement action) cases.

Each agency is created and defined by an "enabling statute" enacted by the Texas state legislature. Generally, the Tex.-APA, Texas Public Information Act (PIA),[8] and the Texas Open Meetings Act[9] set the legal boundaries for conduct of state agencies, boards, and commissions.

State agencies must conform to the mandates found in the U.S. Constitution (primarily due process requirements), the Texas State Constitution,[10] the general provisions of the state General Appropriations Act,[11] requirements for competitive bidding on government purchases, and all other state and federal laws.

The Tex.-APA governs two categories of agency action:

- Adjudication—The Tex.-APA applies when, after an opportunity for an adjudicative (contested, adversarial) hearing, parties' legal rights, duties, or privileges will be affected by agency action. The Tex.-APA sets out the procedures that agencies (and other participants) must follow regarding contested cases (agencies' individual enabling statutes usually define when they must hold hearings).
- Rule making—The Tex.-APA requires formal rule-making activity when agencies intend to implement, interpret, or prescribe law or policy, and outlines procedures agencies must follow in this regard (although, occasionally, agencies may both announce and apply new interpretations of law for the first time in adjudicative hearings).

In addition, Texas has a number of open-government laws that affect administrative procedure, including the following:

Public Information Act

The PIA specifies that agency documents and records are open to the public, absent an express exception. It mandates public access to information that the

---

7. The Texas Constitution and Statutes Home Page, *The Texas Administrative Procedure Act*, www.statutes.legis.state.tx.us; https://www.statutes.legis.state.tx.us/Docs/GV/htm/GV.2001.htm (last visited September 25, 2017).
8. The Texas Attorney General Homepage, *2016 Public Information Handbook*, www.texasattorneygeneral.gov; https://www.texasattorneygeneral.gov/files/og/publicinfo_hb.pdf (last visited September 25, 2017).
9. The Texas Attorney General Homepage, *2016 Open Meetings Handbook*, www.texasattorneygeneral.gov; https://www.texasattorneygeneral.gov/files/og/OMA_handbook_2016.pdf (last visited September 25, 2017).
10. The Texas Constitution and Statutes Home Page, *The Constitution of Texas*, www.constitution.legis.state.tx.us; https://www.constitution.legis.state.tx.us (last visited September 25, 2017).
11. The Legislative Budget Board, *The General Appropriations Act for the 2016-17*, www.lbb.state.tx.us; http://www.lbb.state.tx.us/Documents/GAA/General_Appropriations_Act_2016-2017.pdf (last visited September 25, 2017).

government collects, assembles, or maintains in connection with its transaction of the official business of government bodies.

The PIA contemplates paper documents, recordings, computer files, photographs, and other types of data collection (but not the private information of individuals or threats to public safety). When agencies receive requests for information, the PIA requires them to either disclose the data or seek an attorney general's decision regarding applicability of exceptions to disclosure.

Open Meetings Act

The Open Meetings Act requires that all government bodies, including administrative agencies, deliberate in public meetings (except if a closed or executive session is expressly authorized, such as for personnel matters, real estate negotiations, litigation, and similar sensitive situations). For agencies with state-wide reach, seven days' notice, not including either the date of posting or of the meeting itself, must precede all meetings.

Notices of meetings must be sent to the secretary of state, where they are posted to its website and published every Friday in the Texas Register.[12] The notice must be detailed enough to inform the public of the issues up for debate (including closed-session topics). The greater the expected public interest in a topic, the more specific the details in the notice must be.

Government bodies, including administrative agencies, may not discuss or vote on any point not listed in the meeting's notice.

Florida Administrative Procedure Act

The Florida Administrative Procedure Act (Fla.-APA), which applies only to administrative agencies of the state of Florida, appears in the Florida Statutes at Title 10, Part X, Ch. 120. The Fla.-APA mandates that agencies provide, at least seven days before the event, notice of workshops, public meetings, and hearings through publication on the agency's website and in the Florida Administrative Weekly publication.[13]

Note

The seven-day rule does not apply to emergency actions, according to the Fla.-APA: Emergency exceptions include immediate threats to public health and safety. In an emergency, the Fla.-APA allows agencies to provide public notice through any reasonable procedure that protects the public interest. But in that circumstance, agencies may take only actions that are necessary to protect the public.

---

12. Texas Secretary of State, Welcome to Open Meetings, www.sos.state.tx.us; https://www.sos.state.tx.us/open/index.shtml (last visited September 25, 2017).
13. Fla. Stat. § 120.525.

To serve the public, the Fla.-APA requires that all Florida agencies archive all final orders and provide a searchable subject-matter index. Archive must be available electronically in a public database that is fully searchable and allows retrieval of the full texts of all orders.[14]

The Fla.-APA limits agency authority solely to enacting rules related to the powers and duties granted to the agency by the enabling statute. Agencies may not act to effectuate general statutory provisions related to general legislative intent or overall state policy.[15]

Florida agencies are allowed to grant variances and waivers to secure fair results if petitioners demonstrate that the goal of the underlying statute can be achieved by alternate means. To secure a waiver before an administrative agency, a petitioner must show that the prescribed regulatory procedure creates significant hardship and is fundamentally unfair. In this situation, Florida agencies may adopt a procedure to provide relief.[16]

A committee to review agency rules is required under the Fla.-APA. To uncover invalid delegation of statutory authority, this body examines each proposed rule, accompanying deliberative material, and all emergency rules.[17]

Under the Fla.-APA, the Florida Department of State must publish the Florida Administrative Code on its website. The Florida Administrative Code must include the following:[18]

- All rules and regulations adopted by every agency
- Indices to all administrative rules and regulations
- All historical notes related to adoption of administrative agency rules and regulations
- All other materials that would be useful

Parties alleging that they personally suffered adverse effects from administrative agency rule making may seek declaratory relief relating to enforcement of any statute or agency rule or order.[19] These disputes may be mediated (if mediation is available through the particular agency). But mediation may not affect any party's ultimate right to a hearing before an administrative bench officer.[20]

Professional Licensure Under the Florida Administrative Procedure Act
When individuals apply for professional licenses, Florida state administrative agencies may not deny these applications solely because an applicant failed to

---

14. Fla. Stat. § 120.53.
15. Fla. Stat. § 120.536.
16. Fla. Stat. § 120.542.
17. Fla. Stat. § 120.545.
18. Fla. Stat. § 120.55.
19. Fla. Stat. § 120.565.
20. Fla. Stat. § 120.573.

correct an application error, failed to supply missing data, or failed to supply additional information. Agencies must approve or deny applications within 90 days after receiving the completed application paperwork.[21]

Judicial Review Under the Florida Administrative Procedure Act

In the state of Florida, judicial review is available to parties adversely affected by agency decisions or parties with substantial interest in the matter. The proper venue for judicial review is in the appellate district where the agency has its headquarters, where the party resides, or in any location provided by law. The appellate record must be assembled as prescribed in the Florida Rules of Appellate Procedure.[22] When an agency seeks enforcement of its own actions, the agency must file a petition before the circuit court where the subject matter for enforcement is located.[23]

New York State Administrative Procedure Act

Rule Making

New York state agencies possess powers, delegated by the legislature, that allow them to create rules that regulate particular areas of society. According to the New York State Department of State, New York state agencies perform quasi-legislative functions: they run adversary proceedings between a New York agency and a party that is subject to an agency's regulations. Most agency adversarial hearings relate to whether a regulation has been violated or whether suspending or revoking a professional license or some government benefit is proper.

The State Administrative Procedure Act (N.Y.-SAPA) governs the procedures that most agencies must follow.[24] The N.Y.-SAPA sets out the procedures for how administrative agencies adopt rules and conduct hearings. Under the N.Y.-SAPA, proposed rules (and other agency actions) are published weekly in the New York Register. After adoption, agency rules are published in the New York Codes, Rules, and Regulations (NYCRR). Although agency rules generally must be adopted in accord with the N.Y.-SAPA, the legislature may impose alternate or additional standards.

To propose new rules or to adopt or repeal existing rules, New York state administrative agencies must:

- Publish a notice of proposed rule making in the New York State Register
- Receive and consider comment on the proposed rule
- Formally adopt the rule by publishing in the NYCRR and the New York Register a notice of adoption of the rule

---

21. Fla. Stat. § 120.60.
22. Fla. Stat. § 120.68.
23. Fla. Stat. § 120.68.
24. Found online at: https://www.nysenate.gov/legislation/laws/SAP.

The N.Y.-SAPA includes a highly functional, plain-language overview of rule making in a dynamic subject-matter index, included in the N.Y.-SAPA at Appendix A. Appendix A includes an alphabetized list of major activities and functions, SAPA, executive law, executive orders, and NYCRR citations on every topic.[25]

Getting a Rule Adopted

The N.Y.-SAPA sets out a three-step process for making and amending rules (for nonemergency rules only):[26]

- The new or amended rule is proposed through publication of a notice in the New York State Register.
- Public comment must be solicited and considered.
- The new rule is adopted by filing the full text with the NYCRR, with a Notice of Adoption (for publication in the New York State Register).

Expedited processes allow a Notice of Emergency Adoption to make a rule effective on a temporary basis (a maximum of 90 days from the date filed), without proposing the rule for permanent adoption.

To help navigate rule making under the N.Y.-SAPA, the most common abbreviations are

- ARRC (Administrative Regulations Review Commission), which reviews rule making activities
- DAR (Division of Administrative Rules)
- RRU (Regulatory Review Unit, within the Division of the Budget), which receives and reviews rule-making proposals
- SAPA (State Administrative Procedure Act), which governs the New York rule-making process

Most proposed rules in New York will include the following:

- RIS (Regulatory Impact Statement)
- RFA (Regulatory Flexibility Analysis for Small Businesses and Local Governments)
- RAFA (Rural Area Flexibility Analysis)
- JIS (Job Impact Statement)

When an agency seeks to enforce an existing rule, the affected party has a right to request a hearing; this is a fertile area for counsel to assist clients who are on the receiving end of administrative enforcement activity. The N.Y.-SAPA, at Article 3, sets out extensive rules regarding these adjudicatory proceedings. Article 3 addresses hearings, making and preserving the hearing record, presiding officers

---

25. Appendix A, Subject Index, found online at: https://www.dos.ny.gov/info/rulemakingmanual.html#appa.
26. https://www.dos.ny.gov/info/rulemakingmanual.html.

and their powers, mandatory disclosures, how evidence is handled, and bench officers' decisions and orders.[27] This is the section to which counsel should turn when considering the possibility of representing a client who is challenging an administrative agency action in a hearing before an administrative bench officer.

Administrative hearings for professions and occupations regulated by the New York Department of State are processed through the Office of Administrative Hearings (OAH). The OAH is legally mandated to protect the health, safety, and welfare of the public and to safeguard the due process rights of current licensees and applicants for licensure. This includes real estate brokers, appraisers, notaries public, appearance enhancement professionals, security guards, and private investigators, among many, many others.[28]

Bench officers who hear cases under the N.Y.-SAPA are guided by the Manual for Administrative Law Judges and Hearing Officers, published by the New York State Department of Civil Service.[29] This is a valuable guide for advocates arguing before administrative bench officers presiding over administrative agency hearings.

Other State Administrative Systems

Other busy administrative systems in the United States with well-developed administrative systems include the following:

- Illinois—Ill. Compiled Stat., General Provisions, 5 ILCS 100/, Illinois Administrative Procedure Act[30]
- Pennsylvania—Administrative Procedure Act, Title 2, Pennsylvania Annot. Stat.s[31]
- Ohio—Chapter 119: Administrative Procedure[32]
- Georgia—Georgia Code, Title 50, Ch. 13. Administrative Procedure[33]
- North Carolina—Chapter 150B, Administrative Procedure Act[34]
- Michigan—Michigan Compiled Laws, Administrative Procedures Act of 1969, Act 306[35]
- Puerto Rico—Uniform Administrative Procedure, Title 3, ch. 75. Laws of Puerto Rico, 3 L.P.R.A. § 2101, *et seq.*; when Agencies in Puerto Rico propose to adopt, amend, or repeal rules or regulations, they must publish notices in both Spanish and English, in more than one newspaper of general circulation in Puerto Rico, and on the Internet.[36]

---

27. https://www.nysenate.gov/legislation/laws/SAP/A3.
28. https://www.dos.ny.gov/ooah/index.html.
29. Updated 2011: http://www.wnylc.com/kb_wnylc/entry/15/.
30. Found online at: www.google.com/search?q=Illinois%2C+administrative+procedures+act&oq=Illinois%2C+administrative+procedures+act&aqs=chrome..69i57j0l3.7172j0j7&sourceid=chrome&ie=UTF-8.
31. Found online at: www.legis.state.pa.us/cfdocs/legis/LI/consCheck.cfm?txtType=HTM&ttl=02.
32. Found online at: codes.ohio.gov/orc/119.
33. Found online at: ga.elaws.us/law/50-13.
34. Found online at: www.ncleg.net/EnactedLegislation/Statutes/HTML/ByChapter/Chapter_150B.html.
35. Found online at: www.legislature.mi.gov/documents/mcl/pdf/mcl-act-306-of-1969.pdf.
36. Found online at: https://casetext.com/statute/laws-of-puerto-rico/title-three-executive/chapter-75-uniform-administrative-procedure/subchapter-ii-procedure-for-regulation.

3

Constitutional Limits on Administrative Law

Agencies exercise their power through the right to sanction (fines, revocations, restraints on alienation, disqualifications from some sort of action or activity, and other limitations) within the limit set by the Constitution.[1] A useful objection for counsel to assert on behalf of clients, against administrative agency action, is that the contested sanctions, which might appear to flow from the executive branch,[2] are inconsistent with the constitutional requirement of the separation of powers.

In the United States' representative democracy, which focuses on the idea of three separate branches of government, with each branch checking the exercise of power by the other two, no single branch is allowed to invade any other branch's authority. Separation of powers is a fluid concept, however, and constitutional division of powers arguments are slippery.[3] The reviewing courts determine the degree of intrusion allowed among and between branches of government.

On this basis, resistance to actions effected under ostensible authority of administrative law is rooted in the language of the U.S. Constitution. The Constitution's first substantive words are "All legislative Powers herein granted shall be vested in a Congress of the United States."[4]

---

1. The U.S. Supreme Court recognized that agencies exercise judicial powers when they impose and enforce monetary penalties (*Oceanic Steam Navigation Co. v. Stranahan*, 214 U.S. 320 (1909)).
2. Almost all agencies are executive agencies and are part of the executive branch of government.
3. *United States Constitution*, www.archives.gov; https://www.archives.gov/founding-docs/constitution-transcript (last visited September 25, 2017).
4. *United States Constitution*, www.archives.gov; https://www.archives.gov/founding-docs/constitution-transcript (last visited September 25, 2017).

Administrative agencies' courts lack the procedural protections guaranteed by the Constitution.[5] Administrative adjudication uses subordinate judges, ignores jury participation, cannot convene grand juries, and might not include protection against self-incrimination.

Despite numerous challenges and objections, administrative law and adjudication have expanded, as government itself has expanded, likely corresponding to American life generally becoming more complex.[6] But this expansion triggered some challenges of its own, including restraining government power by limiting its delegation, monitoring the use of power, and providing adequate review of the use of power. These are all useful approaches for counsel to explore when representing individuals who are fighting government administrative actions.

Delegating Government Rule-Making Power: What NOT to Do

A barrier to understanding administrative law is Congress' power to delegate its legislative power to administrative agencies (Article I, Section I, U.S. Constitution: all legislative power is vested in Congress[7]). The U.S. Supreme Court long ago recognized Congress' right to delegate legislative authority to agencies, but only so long as the scope of agency discretion is clearly constrained by Congress.[8]

On this basis, courts strike laws that invest too much legislative power in administrative agencies.[9] So when Congress delegates authority to administrative agencies, it details procedures to block arbitrary action by these agencies. Courts look for these procedural safeguards against arbitrary actions or enforcement abuses by agencies when engaged in judicial review of administrative agency decisions.

Generally, once an administrative agency alleges that a violation has occurred or exists, the agency must provide to respondents the right to notice of the charges and either the right to be heard at an agency hearing or the right to challenge the agency's determination in court.[10]

---

5. Opponents of administrative agency adjudication argue that the process does not answer fully enough to the U.S. Constitution's Bill of Rights.

6. Scholars date the origination of administrative law from 1887, when Congress authorized the Interstate Commerce Commission. The prevalence of administrative law has expanded as Congress created more administrative agencies. State administrative agencies frequently mirror federal activities, so states' administrative structures expanded along similar lines.

7. Found online at: https://www.usconstitution.net/xconst_A1Sec1.html.

8. Courts have set limits on the delegation of judicial functions to administrative agencies: Congress may not delegate to administrative executive officers the power to set criminal penalties or to define the scope of their application; only district court judges may do this.

9. Regarding how much delegation of power to administrative agencies the U.S. Supreme Court can tolerate, two cases discuss Franklin D. Roosevelt's New Deal programs: *Panama Refining Co. v. Ryan*, 293 U.S. 388 (1935) and *Schecter Poultry Corp. v. U.S.*, 295 U.S. 495 (1935). U.S. Supreme Court Chief Justice John Marshall, recognizing that the executive branch needed regulatory powers to implement the law, stated that government officials administering statutory programs must be permitted to "fill up the details" (*Wayman v. Southard*, 23 U.S. 1, 36 (1825)). On grounds of over-broad delegation of legislative power, legislation regulating prices and labor relations in the coal industry was unconstitutional (*Carter v. Carter Coal Co.*, 298 U.S. 238 (1936)). Although delegations have broadened, no federal transfer of legislative power has recently been ruled unconstitutional.

10. The "very essence of civil liberty certainly consists of the right of every individual to claim the protection of the laws, whenever he receives an injury," U.S. Supreme Court Chief Justice John Marshall wrote. He warned that a government cannot be called a "government of laws, and not of men . . . . if the laws furnish no remedy for the violation of a vested legal right." (*Marbury v. Madison*, 5 U.S. 137 (1803)).

4

How Administrative Agencies
Create Law

How Federal Agencies Generate Bodies of Law

The federal APA (FAPA, adopted in 1947) sets out the process that federal administrative agencies must use when they draft rules and regulations, then seek to enact them. Both executive and independent federal agencies must follow the rule-making procedures of the FAPA. It provides standards for formal adjudication at administrative hearings by agencies and describes situations in which courts may review and nullify agency rules.

This is useful for counsel both challenging and defending administrative agency actions concerning these rules and regulations.

The Rule-Making Process

The FAPA ensures that the public receives notice of proposed laws and has an opportunity to respond to those proposed laws. It ensures that subsequent administrative rule making follows the prescribed process:

- Agencies must publish proposed rules in the Federal Register.
- The public must have at least 45 days to review the rules and submit comments (public comments can oppose or support a proposed rule).
- Individuals, companies, and interest groups (just about anyone) can submit comments.

The FAPA requires agencies to summarize and respond to each public comment, and each comment is available to the public as part of the rule-making record. During the 45-day comment period, agencies may hold public hearings, but if an agency elects not to, anyone can submit a written request for a hearing at least 15 days before the close of the public review period.

Agencies must review the comments they receive and consider changes in response. Depending on how broad the new rule's reach is, the agency may be required to allow the public 15 days for comment on the amended version. This cycle may happen a few times before the rule reaches its early final form.

Oversight of Federal Rule Making

The Federal Office of Administrative Law (OAL) oversees federal agency rule making. Agencies must send to the OAL, within one year from the date of release to the public, the text of any proposed rule. To determine whether the agency complied with the FAPA, the OAL reviews the law and the procedures the agency used. If the agency's actions followed the FAPA, it is allowed to complete the rule-making process: it can publish a final rule.

The final version of the new rule is printed in the Federal Register and the Code of Federal Regulations. Counsel can then cite to, rely on, and argue the new rule.[1]

Example: U.S. Territories

Puerto Rico

Puerto Rico follows the Uniform Administrative Procedure (Title 3, Ch. 75, Laws of Puerto Rico).[2] Agencies in Puerto Rico must establish rules and procedures for the informal resolution of matters submitted for their consideration.[3]

Judicial review of agency decisions is available. Any party adversely affected by a final order or resolution of an agency, and who has exhausted all the remedies provided by the agency, may file a petition for review with the court of appeals. This appeal must be filed within 30 days of the date that the copy of the notice of the order or final resolution was filed in the agency's records.[4]

Parties adversely affected by the court of appeals decision may seek review by filing a petition for a writ of certiorari with the Supreme Court of Puerto Rico.[5]

---

1. *A Guide to the Rulemaking Process* (prepared by the Office of the Federal Register), found online at: www .federalregister.gov/uploads/2011/01/the_rulemaking_process.pdf.
2. Found online via Lexis Advance at: advance.lexis.com/container?config=0151JABiZDY4NzhiZS1hN2 IxLTRlYzUtOTg3Yi1hNzIxN2RlMDM1ZDIKAFBvZENhdGFsb2eo3IN9q6nyuOdhcatJGdcs&crid=dbcc7 c0d-684d-4607-b390-0e17cf80a4d1.
3. 3 L.P.R.A. § 2101.
4. 3 L.P.R.A. § 2172.
5. 3 L.P.R.A. § 2177.

> **Guam**
> In Guam, administrative law and procedure is found in the Administrative Adjudication Law,[6] codified at 5 GCA Government Operations, Ch. 9: Administrative Adjudication Law.[7] Article 1 addresses definitions, Article 2 includes General Provisions, and Article 3 prescribes Rule-Making Procedures.

How State Agencies Generate Bodies of Law

Counsel attacking or defending an agency's attempts at rule making or enforcement of those rules or regulations can examine the agency's processes for useful facts regarding its conduct. If the agency arguably implemented a rule beyond its legislative mandate, this could be grounds for overturning the rule or regulation. Conversely, strict adherence to prescribed rule-making methods and constitutional soundness help agency counsel fend off a challenge to the agency's authority. All of this is foundational to counsel's successful representation of clients in administrative litigation.

Example: California

The Cal.-APA[8] mandates how agencies adopt regulations (most U.S. states and territories run similar, but not identical, processes: counsel should check processes for their particular state or territory). The Cal.-APA created California's Office of Administrative Law (the OAL), which reviews proposed regulations for necessity. In each proposed regulation's Initial Statement of Reasons, paperwork must describe the need for each proposed provision.

The Cal.-APA limits agencies to regulations within their scope of authority (found in their enabling statutes) that are consistent with state laws and do not conflict with federal laws. It provides for public participation in the rule-making process: interested people or organizations must be allowed to petition to modify, adopt, amend, or repeal a regulation (absent other restrictions). An agency's refusal to allow public participation, absent extraordinary circumstances, can be a basis for counsel to argue that the objectionable rule is generally unenforceable, including, specifically, to counsel's client.

Regulations include rules, orders, and standards of general application, as well as amendments, supplements, or revision of any rule, regulation, order, or standard adopted by any state agency to implement, interpret, or make specific the law enforced or administered by the enabling statute.

---

6. GC § 24000.
7. Found online at: www.guamcourts.org/CompilerofLaws/GCA/05gca/5gc009.PDF.
8. The California Administrative Procedure Act (Cal. Gov't. Code §§ 11340-11365).

The OAL's goal for all California agencies is regulations that are clear, necessary, and legally sound. The Cal.-APA offers three avenues for adoption of agency directives:

- Regular
- Emergency
- Underground regulations (the petition process)

The rule-making process used by an agency to adopt regulations dictates the procedural requirements, including the rule-making record, timeframes, public participation, the OAL's review, and the effective dates for regulations.

Many agencies promulgate numerous binding policies and procedures addressing their internal administrative processes. These policies and procedures develop into regulations that appear in the state or federal Code of Regulations.

Regular Rule-Making Process

Agencies create the documents required to conduct formal Cal.-APA rule making. Some agencies involve the public at this step; others do not. If the proposed new rule is extensive or complicated, agencies *must* engage in prenotification public discussions (workshopping).[9] During this phase, agencies must develop four documents:

1. The proposed text
2. The Initial Statement of Reasons
3. The form STD. 399 Fiscal Impact Statement
4. The Notice of Proposed Regulatory Action (Notice)

To start rule making, agencies issue notices by publication in the Regulatory Notice Register.[10] They must mail notices to individuals or entities that filed Requests for Notice of Regulatory Action. Agencies post the notice, text, and Initial Statement of Reasons on their websites.[11]

After publication in the Register, the rule-making process time clock begins to count down; agencies have one year to finish the rule making and send the file to the OAL. The Cal.-APA requires a minimum of 45 days for public comments. Notices must specify the deadline and address for receiving written comments.

Although, under the Cal.-APA, agencies are not required to hold public hearings on proposed new rules, if they do not, any entity may request it. Requests must be submitted at least 15 days before the close of the written public comment

---

9. Cal. Gov't. Code § 11346.45.
10. Cal. Ofc. of Admin. Law, California Regulatory Notice Register, www.ola.gov.ca; https://oal.ca.gov/publications/notice_register (last visited September 25, 2017).
11. Cal. Gov't. Code § 11346.5.

period; if a request is received, the agency must give notice of and hold hearings.[12] After public comments, agencies may change their proposals. The agency then determines whether the change fits one of the following categories:

- Nonsubstantial
- Substantial and sufficiently related
- Substantial and not sufficiently related[13]

Agencies must entertain public comment for each substantial, sufficiently related change to its proposed rule, at least 15 days before adopting the new rule. For this reason, if agencies adopt these changes, they must mail notices of opportunity to comment on proposed modifications, with a copy of the text of the new proposed changes, to each person who submitted written comments on the proposal, testified at the public hearing, or asked to receive a Notice of Proposed Modifications. Agencies must post the notice(s) on their websites, but hearings are not required (the public may send written comments).

Agencies must consider comments directed to the proposed modifications received during the 15-day comment period; they may conduct multiple 15-day comment periods. They must summarize and respond (on the record) to timely comments about the proposal or the agency's procedures during the regulatory action. With each comment, the agency must either explain how it changed the proposed new rule to reflect the comment, or explain its reasons for not changing the proposal.

The agency's summary and response to comments are part of the complete rule-making file in the Final Statement of Reasons.[14] Agencies must send new rules to the OAL for review within one year from the date the agency published its notice in the Regulatory Notice Register. The OAL has 30 working days[15] to review an agency's rule-making record. The OAL ensures that agencies' actions are procedurally sufficient under the Cal.-APA and reviews proposed new rules for compliance with the six legal standards of the Cal.-APA:

- Authority
- Reference
- Consistency
- Clarity
- Nonduplication
- Necessity

---

12. Cal. Gov't. Code § 11346.8.
13. Cal. Gov't. Code § 11346.8(c).
14. Cal. Gov't. Code § 11346.9.
15. Excludes weekends, holidays, court holidays, and days of emergency closure.

Regarding the substantive content of the regulations, however, the OAL may not substitute its judgment for that of the agency.[16]

Although this sounds complicated, agencies are experienced in this process. However, an agency's failure to follow these processes can undermine enforceability of the rule or regulation, especially as applied to counsel's client: this is an area for counsel to defend a client against an agency's enforcement attempts and also a basis to argue constitutional sufficiency in defense of agency enforcement.

Emergency Rule-Making

Agencies may adopt emergency rules to avoid serious harm to the public peace, health, safety, or general welfare; or if a statute designates a situation an emergency under the Cal.-APA. Emergency rule-making processes are short. The OAL reviews emergency rules for compliance with the Cal.-APA's emergency rule-making requirements.

> ### Note
>
> To meet these requirements, California agencies should choose an effective date and count backward at least 17 days to calendar emergency rule-making compliance deadlines.

At least five working days (not holidays, weekends, or periods of emergency closure of government offices) before filing with the OAL, agencies must mail out and post an emergency notice (the five-day notice is not required if it is a Government Code § 11346.1(a)(3) emergency).[17] The five-day notice must include the following:

- Proposed text
- Finding of emergency (including one California Code of Regulations § 48 statement[18])
- Justification of emergency (narrative)
- Government Code § 11346.5(a)(2)(6) information[19]

---

16. Cal. Gov't. Code § 11349.1.

17. Agencies need not provide the five-day notice if the emergency clearly poses an immediate, serious harm for which delaying action to allow public comment would not serve the public interest.

18. Unless the emergency situation clearly poses such an immediate, serious harm where delaying action to allow public comment would be inconsistent with the public interest, the notice required by Gov't. Code § 11346.1(a) shall contain the following (or substantially similar) statement: "Government Code § 11346.1(a)(2) requires that, at least five working days before submission of the proposed emergency action to the Office of Administrative Law, the adopting agency provide a notice of the proposed emergency action to every person who has filed a request for notice . . . After submission . . . to the Office of Administrative Law, the Office . . . shall allow interested persons five calendar days to submit comments . . . (Gov't. Code §§ 11349.6, 11342.4, 11342.545, 11346.1).

19. This refers to the authority under which the regulation is proposed and the particular code sections (or other provisions of law) being implemented, interpreted, or made specific. Cal. Gov't. Code, Title 2, Div. 3 (Executive Department), Part 1 (State Departments and Agencies), Ch. 3.5 (Administrative Regulations and Rulemaking), Art. 5 (Public Participation: Procedure for Adoption of Regulations); found online at: http://leginfo.legislature .ca.gov/faces/codes_displaySection.xhtml?lawCode=GOV&sectionNum=11346.5.

At least 10 calendar days (not working days) before the target effective date of the new emergency regulation, agencies must file emergency rule-making documents with the OAL. The agency's filing with the OAL must include the following:

- Form STD. 400 (plus six additional copies)[20]
- Proposed text (plus six additional copies)
- Form STD. 399[21]
- Finding of emergency (narrative)
- One CCR § 50(a)(5)(A) statement[22]

During the first five days of the OAL's review, the public may submit comments, with a copy to the agency (absent a Government Code § 11346.1(a)(3) emergency,[23] in which case, public comments will not be considered).

Agencies generally have until the eighth day of the OAL's 10-day review period to respond to public comments (this is not mandatory). The OAL's deadline for a decision is the tenth day after the agency files the proposed emergency rule with the OAL. If the OAL approves the rule, this is the OAL's deadline for filing the approved new emergency rule with California's secretary of state.

If the OAL approves the emergency rule, it is effective once the OAL files with the secretary of state; the emergency rule is effective for 180 days after filing. Up to two 90-day re-adoptions are allowed if the agency is moving to adopt similar, permanent regulations.[24] To convert emergency regulations into permanent ones, California agencies must conduct regular rule making, including notice and comment periods (Certificate of Compliance documentation is required). Failure to do so could be a basis to argue against enforcement of an administrative agency's proposed action against counsel's client.

Although this discussion focuses on California, which has the busiest administrative rule-making and adjudication apparatus of any state in the United States, other states and territories follow vaguely similar procedures, focused on notice and comment opportunities, with limited emergency implementations allowed.

---

20. Cal. Ofc. of Admin. Law, Form STD. 400; found online at: www.ola.gov.ca: https://www.oal.ca.gov/wp-content/uploads/sites/28/2017/05/Std_Form_400_rev_1-2013_apprvd_final_final.pdf (last visited September 25, 2017.

21. Cal. Ofc. of Admin. Law, Form STD. 399; found online at: www.ola.gov.ca, https://www.documents.dgs.ca.gov/dgs/fmc/pdf/std399.pdf (last visited September 25, 2017).

22. Proposed Emergency Action Submission (1 Code of California Regulations (CCR) § 50). State agencies submitting emergency regulations to the Cal. OAL under Gov't. Code § 11346.1 shall include:*** (5)(A) A statement by the submitting Agency confirming that it has complied with the requirement to provide Notice of proposed rulemaking action under Gov't. Code § 11346.1(a)(2)....

23. Agencies are not required to provide notice if the emergency situation clearly poses such an immediate, serious harm that delaying action to allow public comment would be inconsistent with the public interest (Gov't. Code § 11346.1(a)(3)).

24. Different states' APAs allow for different lengths of time for effectiveness of emergency rules and permission to re-adopt as an emergency rule. Counsel should read the particular state APA that controls counsel's client's matter.

California Underground Regulations

If an agency issues, uses, enforces, or attempts to enforce a rule without correctly following the Cal.-APA (if required), the rule is an underground regulation. Agencies may not enforce underground regulations; rather, they must adopt regulations following the Cal.-APA. If counsel believes that a California state agency has an underground regulation, counsel may challenge it.

To challenge an underground regulation, counsel must file a petition with the OAL (the OAL website explains the process).[25] If the OAL accepts the petition, it may issue a determination.[26] The OAL's review of underground regulations to decide whether the alleged underground regulation must be implemented as a regulation under the Cal.-APA is limited to deciding whether the policy or procedure is either a rule or standard of general application, or a modification or supplement to such a rule.

The OAL considers whether the policy or procedure has been adopted by an agency to implement, interpret, or make specific the law enforced or administered by the agency or to govern the agency's procedure. If so, the rule is an underground regulation under California law. But if the regulation is merely a restatement of the law, it is not a new rule.

Next, the OAL must consider whether the regulation is expressly exempted by statute from the requirement of the Cal.-APA (generally, regulations of state agencies must be implemented under the Cal.-APA, unless expressly exempted by statute[27]). If the underground regulation is not expressly exempted, the mandatory rule-making requirements of the Cal.-APA apply.[28]

Agencies using underground regulations must certify in writing to the secretary of state that they have stopped using the underground regulation. The OAL pursues numerous agencies every year for underground regulation violations.[29] Counsel's advocacy for clients in this regard is not a waste of time.

---

25. The OAL is located at: California Office of Administrative Law, 300 Capitol Mall, #1250, Sacramento, CA 95814. California Office of Administrative Law, Petition Explanation and Instructions, www.ola.gov.ca; https://www.oal.ca.gov/wp-content/uploads/sites/28/2017/05/Petition-Explanation-and-Instructions.pdf (last visited September 25, 2017). California Office of Administrative Law, Petition Flowchart Graphic, www.ola.gov.ca, https://www.oal.ca.gov/wp-content/uploads/sites/28/2017/05/Underground-Regs-Petition-Process_FINALFI-NAL_for_Website_Post_June-2014.pdf (last visited September 25, 2017). California Office of Administrative Law, Optional Petition Submission Form, www.ola.gov.ca, https://www.oal.ca.gov/wp-content/uploads/sites/28/2017/05/Optional-petition.pdf (last visited September 25, 2017).
26. California Office of Administrative Law, California Code of Regulations, Title 1, Chapter 2, www.ola.gov.ca, https://www.oal.ca.gov/wp-content/uploads/sites/28/2017/05/CTU-Section250etseqJuly9effective.pdf (last visited September 25, 2017).
27. Cal. Gov't. Code § 11346.
28. If litigation challenging an alleged underground regulation has already been initiated, a determination issued by the OAL in this regard may not be argued to the court in the pending litigation (Gov't. Code § 11340.5(e)).
29. Cal. Ofc. Admin. Law, Underground Regulation Determinations; found online at: www.ola.gov.ca; https://oal.ca.gov/publications/underground_regulation_determinations (last visited September 25, 2017).

The Department of Corrections: Dealing with Underground Regulations

The OAL prosecutes violations of the California Department of Corrections and Rehabilitation (CDCR) regarding underground regulations.[30] The OAL looks for evidence in documents written or issued by the CDCR that affect inmates or classes of inmates statewide.

The OAL requires the following:

- The rule must be in a written document (Code of Reg., Title 1, § 260).
- The rule must be generally applicable (prison "local rules" are exempt from the Cal.-APA). A rule that is adopted and enforced by an individual institution is a local rule, not an underground regulation (Cal. Pen. Code § 5058(c)).[31]

For petitions challenging alleged underground regulation of the CDCR, send correspondence to both the OAL and the CDCR, at the Regulations and Policy Management Branch, California Department of Corrections and Rehabilitation, P.O. Box 942883, Sacramento, CA 94283-0001.

Example: Texas

The Tex.-APA focuses on ensuring minimum standards for uniform practice and procedure for state administrative agencies, providing for public participation in rule making, and clarifying the contours of judicial review of state agency action.[32] Agencies must adopt rules of practice: they must publish rules, statements of policy, final orders, decisions, and opinions. These must all be publicly accessible.[33]

The public may petition Texas agencies to request adoption of rules.[34] Within 60 days of receipt of a petition for rule making, agencies may deny the petition in writing, stating its reasons for the denial, or initiate a responsive rule-making proceeding.

---

30. The OAL does not consider disputes between inmates and their institutions over how regulations adopted under the Cal.-APA are applied; the CDCR uses an administrative inmate appeal process for this. The OAL does not hear appeals of matters that have gone through that process.
31. Pen. Code § 5058(c): The following are not regulations under Gov't. Code § 11342.600: (1) Rules . . . applying solely to a particular prison . . ., provided that . . .: (A) All rules that apply to prisons . . . are adopted by the director pursuant to Ch. 3.5 (commencing with § 11340) of Gov't. Code Part 1, Division 3, Title 2. (B) All rules, unless excluded . . . pursuant to subdivision (f) of Gov't. Code § 6254 are made available to all inmates . . . to which the rules apply and to all members of the general public. (2) Short-term criteria for the placement of inmates . . . planned for closing during its last six months of operation, provided that the criteria are made available . . . and that an estimate of fiscal impact is completed (§§ 6650-6670, incl.), of the State Admin. Manual. (3) Rules issued by the director that are excluded . . . pursuant to Gov't. Code § 6254(f).
32. Texas Administrative Procedures Act, Tex. Gov't. Code Title 10, Ch. 2001 (Tex. Gov't. Code § 2001.001, *et seq.*).
33. See Tex. Gov't. Code § 2001.004.
34. See Tex. Gov't. Code § 2001.021.

Note
If a Texas agency determines that a proposed rule may affect a local economy, it must prepare a local employment impact statement.[35]

Regular Rule Making

Texas agencies must give at least 30 days' notice to the Texas secretary of state of an intent to adopt a rule, before taking a final action;[36] at the same time, they must send a copy of the Notice of Proposed Rule to the lieutenant governor and speaker of the House of Representatives. Agencies must then post their rule-making plans online and publish them in the Texas Register.

Before adopting proposed new rules, agencies must extend to the public a reasonable opportunity to submit data, share views, or make arguments (either orally or in writing).[37] Agencies must set public hearings before adopting any substantive rules, and they must consider all written and oral submissions.

To gather opinions and advice from the public about proposed rule making, Texas agencies may legally use informal conferences or consultations.[38] In addition, agencies may form committees to advise them about contemplated rule making; members may include subject-matter experts, interested individuals, or any combination of these.

When a Texas agency proposes to adopt final rules, it must state the reasons (both for and against) adoption.[39] Before proposed agency rules can be adopted, they are referred to the proper standing legislative committee for review.[40]

Counsel arguing against adoption or enforcement of agency rules might find useful material if an agency skipped a step or missed a deadline, especially if it prejudices to counsel's client. Agency counsel will argue either that the agency met all its rule-making procedural and substantive obligations or, if it didn't, that the failure is de minimis, especially as to counsel's client.

Counsel attacking enforcement of agency rules against counsel's client should be prepared to argue constitutional violations resulting in prejudice. This argument, backed up by a few facts, could get a court to order a stay or even overturn the objectionable rule. Considering this potential argument, counsel might get the agency to back off enforcement of counsel's client for a period of time, allowing for a negotiated resolution.

---

35. See Tex. Gov't. Code § 2001.022.
36. See Tex. Gov't. Code § 2001.023.
37. See Tex. Gov't. Code § 2001.029.
38. See Tex. Gov't. Code § 2001.031.
39. See Tex. Gov't. Code § 2001.030.
40. See Tex. Gov't. Code § 2001.032.

Emergency Rule Making

Texas agencies may adopt emergency rules when they find that an immediate danger to the public health, safety, or welfare requires adoption of a rule with fewer than 30 days' notice (agencies must state in writing the bases for their findings in this regard).[41] These emergency rules remain in effect no longer than 120 days.

Texas State Office of Administrative Hearings

The Texas State Office of Administrative Hearings (the SOAH) is neutral and independent. It conducts hearings and mediations in response to referrals from state agencies. It is an independent agency of the state's executive branch. The SOAH neither advocates for nor crafts policy.

The SOAH's mission is to conduct fair, prompt, and efficient hearings and mediations and provide fair, reasoned, and timely decisions. Generally, absent a contrary mandate, proposed and final decisions must be issued not later than 60 days after the record closes.[42]

Mediation is collaborative and confidential; it provides an opportunity to resolve disputes without formal administrative hearings. The SOAH uses formal mediation to resolve contested matters.[43] Through assisted negotiations, mediators facilitate communication between the parties to achieve a mutually acceptable resolution; the parties themselves determine whether and on what terms their dispute is resolved.

If mediation is not successful, the Texas Administrative Procedures Act provides that the parties retain the right to an administrative hearing before an administrative judge who did not participate in the mediation.

Example: Florida

The state of Florida has approximately 50 administrative agencies; the Florida Administrative Procedure Act (the Fla.-APA) is found at Florida Statutes, Title 10, Part X, Chapter 120. All of these agencies promulgate rules and

---

41. See Tex. Gov't. Code § 2001.034.

42. As an example of timelines calculations interrupted by emergency closures of government offices, the following notice appeared, after Hurricane Harvey hit the region, on the welcome page of the Texas State Office of Administrative Hearings (with no explanation of how this affects the administrative process): "Hurricane Closures & Cancellations – UPDATE: SOAH's Houston field office is presently closed and will reopen at a later date to be announced. The cancellation of all hearings in the Houston office has been extended from September 15, 2017, to September 22, 2017. We will advise at a later date regarding the status of hearings that are set beyond September 22, 2017. Please continue to monitor SOAH's website for information."

Compare the following notice from the Financial Industry Regulatory Agency dispute resolution portal regarding closures in Puerto Rico after that territory was hit by a hurricane: Hurricane Maria's Impact on Puerto Rico: Due to Hurricane Maria's impact on Puerto Rico, FINRA Office of Dispute Resolution is administratively canceling all hearings and conference calls scheduled to be held on or before October 6, 2017 in cases venued in Puerto Rico. FINRA will begin the process of rescheduling any impacted hearings or pre-hearings as soon as reasonably practicable. Similarly, all case related deadlines including, but not limited to, answers, arbitrator rankings, and motions falling on or before October 6, 2017 in cases venued in Puerto Rico are administratively extended to October 13, 2017 . . .

43. The SOAH's procedural rules concerning mediation are codified at 1 Tex. Admin. Code § 155.351.

act to enforce these rules through the agencies' power to issue and enforce citations.[44]

The contours of a Florida agency's enabling statute set out the powers and duties that limit the rules it may adopt. Agencies may not, however, adopt rules solely because they are reasonably related to the overall purpose of the relevant legislation.[45]

The Florida Administrative Code (the Florida Code) contains all rules adopted by all Florida agencies, including all historical notes, indexes to all rules, and other materials. The Department of State must post the Florida Code on its website.[46] Agencies must compile public, searchable, electronic databases of the full texts of all agency orders, including a subject-matter index.[47]

Florida agencies must publish notices of public meetings, hearings, and workshops in the Florida Administrative Weekly and on the particular agency's website at least seven days before the event (except emergency meetings).[48] Agencies can set emergency meetings in cases of imminent danger to public health, safety, and welfare. In emergencies, agencies may give notice through reasonable procedures that protect the public interest. In an emergency, agencies may only take actions that are necessary to protect the public.

When strict application of the rule-making procedures leads to unfair results, Florida state agencies may adopt procedures to grant variances and waivers. Relief is appropriate if the goals of the underlying statute can be achieved by other means, the existing procedure works as a hardship, and it violates principles of fairness.[49] When agency rule making affects an individual or other entity, the individual or entity may seek declaratory relief[50] related to the applicability of any statutory provision, rule, or order of an agency.[51]

If mediation is available for that type of administrative action, the matter might be resolvable through mediation, but mediation never interferes with or preempts a party's right to a hearing.[52]

---

44. Found online at: www.google.com/search?q=Florida+Statutes%2C+Title+10%2C+Part+X%2C+Chapter+120&oq=Florida+Statutes%2C+Title+10%2C+Part+X%2C+Chapter+120&aqs=chrome.. 69i57.574j0j4&sourceid=chrome&ie=UTF-8.
45. Fla. Stat. § 120.536.
46. Fla. Stat. § 120.55.
47. Fla. Stat. § 120.53.
48. Fla. Stat. § 120.525.
49. Fla. Stat. § 120.542.
50. Declaratory relief is a judicial determination of the parties' rights under a statute (a "declaratory judgment"— definition found online at: dictionary.law.com/Default.aspx?selected=448).
51. Fla. Stat. § 120.565.
52. Fla. Stat. § 120.573.

Professional Licensure and the Florida Administrative Procedures Act

When an applicant for a professional license in the state of Florida submits application materials, agencies may approve or deny applications within 90 days after receiving a completed submission.[53] Agencies may not deny licenses because the applicant failed to correct an error or failed to supply information.

Florida Agency Action: Judicial Review and Enforcement

Under § 120.68 of Title X, any entity adversely affected by an agency decision is entitled (with some exceptions) to judicial review in Florida's District Court of Appeal[54] in an appropriate venue. Entities with significant interests in matters before Florida agencies may, in some instances, be entitled to file enforcement petitions in the Florida District Courts of Appeal.[55]

In general, if an administrative bench officer's final order turns on the officer's factual finding, the appellate district court may not substitute its judgment for that of the administrative bench officer regarding the weight of the evidence on any disputed finding of fact. However, if the appellate district court finds that the administrative bench officer's final order depends on a factual finding not supported by competent, substantial evidence in the official record of the proceeding, the appellate court must either set aside the final order or remand the case to the administrative bench officer.[56]

This analysis provides a roadmap for counsel's arguments regarding either securing appellate review or fending off an attempt at securing review. Counsel can argue that the administrative bench officer's decision either focuses predominantly on factual findings or is beyond the administrative bench officer's argument in support of the decision. This determination is more slippery than might be expected and can in some instances provide enough momentum to secure court review of the client's matter.

Agencies must ensure that their rules conform with related statutory requirements. The Fla.-APA does not repeal any statute that secures a party's right to be heard in a circuit court or cancel the circuit court's jurisdiction to render declaratory judgments.

---

53. Fla. Stat. § 120.60
54. The state of Florida has five District Courts of Appeal, each comprising multi-judge panels; they review lower court decisions for harmful error.
55. Fla. Stat. § 120.68. Each of Florida's circuit courts (courts of general jurisdiction) serves one of the 20 judicial circuits (www.flcourts.org/Florida-Courts-Trial-Courts-Circuit).
56. www.leg.state.fl.us/Statutes/index.cfm?App_mode=Display_Statute&Search_String=&URL=0100-0199/0120/Sections/0120.68.html.

Example: New York

The New York State Administrative Procedure Act (SAPA)[57] contains five sections: Article 1, General Provisions; Article 2, Rule Making; Article 3, Adjudicatory Proceedings; Article 4, Licenses; and Article 5, Representation.[58]

The SAPA dictates a straightforward, uniform administrative procedure. To accomplish this, the SAPA requires that, before adopting rules, agencies submit notices of proposed rule making for publication in the state register.[59] Agencies must offer the public a chance to submit comments. When agencies file rules with the New York secretary of state, they must submit a notice of adoption for publication in the state register.[60]

Administrative agency rules become effective when the agency files them with the New York secretary of state and the notice of adoption is published in the state's register. After an agency files a rule with the secretary of state, the agency may amend, suspend, or repeal the new rule before its effective date.[61]

In response to a petition, the SAPA requires agencies to issue declaratory rulings with respect to the applicability of any rule regarding enforcement related to any person, property, or set of facts; and determine whether any particular action should be taken pursuant to a rule.[62]

This mandate is helpful to counsel representing clients affected by a New York agency's enforcement action; counsel can use this as free legal research and possibly free discovery. Strategically drafted petitions could test the limits of the rules in question and provide comparison data that could be useful for counsel's advocacy.

In most proceedings, responsive data from the agency itself will be powerful ammunition in the agency's own administrative hearing venue as well as in judicial review by a court. At the very least, it could negate the arguments of agency counsel; this can be determinative, depending on the burden of proof in that venue.

The SAPA prescribes that New York agencies will offer hearings regarding their enforcement actions. In adjudicatory proceedings, all parties must be afforded an opportunity for reasonably timely hearings.

---

57. Found online at: https://www.nysenate.gov/legislation/laws/SAP/204.
58. Highlights of the SAPA include Article 1 General Provisions § 100 et seq. setting out the legislative intent; § 102 Definitions, including "Agency" (public authority . . . authorized by law to make rules or to make final decisions in adjudicatory proceedings and "Rule" (agency statement, regulation or code of general applicability that implements or applies law, or prescribes a fee charged by or paid to any agency); Article 2 Rule Making (each agency shall strive to ensure that . . . documents are written in a clear and coherent manner; and agencies may adopt emergency rules.
59. NY St. Admin. P. Act § 202; Agencies are directed to submit rule-making notices to the governor, the senate president pro tempore, the speaker of the assembly, the administrative regulations review commission, and the office of regulatory and management assistance at the time the agency submits its notice to the New York secretary of state for publication in the state register.
60. The SAPA requires that agencies develop proposed new rules and work to avoid negative economic impacts or other too-burdensome effects (NY St. Admin. P. Act § 202-a).
61. This is true unless this results in a substantial revision of the rule as proposed for adoption (NY St. Admin. P. Act § 203).
62. NY St. Admin. P. Act § 204.

If counsel believes that his or her client was denied reasonably prompt access to the agency's administrative hearing apparatus, counsel can lodge an objection to the validity of the proceeding at the start of the hearing and move to administratively dismiss all citations or fines or both (or negate fees and fines that have been multiplied through the passage of time).

The administrative bench officer likely will take the matter under submission and might never rule on it at all. Either way, counsel has lodged and preserved the point for appellate advocacy, if needed.

Agencies are empowered to conduct adjudicatory proceedings; as a corollary, they are directed to adopt appropriate rules outlining discovery (including depositions).[63]

All parties must be allowed to offer factual evidence and make legal arguments at hearings before designated hearing officers.[64] Participants appearing before any agency adjudicatory body may be represented by counsel.[65] The decisions and orders of the agency must be in writing and include findings of fact and reasons that support the ultimate determination.[66] The SAPA provides for judicial review of agency rules; counsel can secure this right through petition or request for declaratory judgment.

Conclusion

These overviews of the California, Texas, Florida, and New York Administrative Procedure Acts are examples that show the level of detail to which agencies must adhere to effectively and legally produce rules, regulations, and other requirements to support the agencies' enforcement and citation powers.

Counsel both attacking agency enforcement and defending agency citations should compare the specific agency's path to final rule making with the particular state's APA requirements to find an opening for a constitutional due process or other argument to get the agency's attention and forward the client's case.

Most U.S. states and territories and the federal government follow similar processes, but the devil is always in the details. Counsel must understand the particular details of the applicable state's APA. But court precedential analyses regarding administrative law issues can often be applied across state and territorial lines.

Counsel should skim the particular state's minimum hearing requirements and compare these to the actual agency hearing process. Counsel should note and argue failures on the record and consider making related due process, constitutional, and other arguments in appellate proceedings, if any.

---

63. NY St. Admin. P. Act § 305.
64. NY St. Admin. P. Act §§ 301, 303.
65. NY St. Admin. P. Act § 501.
66. NY St. Admin. P. Act § 307.

5

State and Federal Administrative Agency Power

Once the government approves a regulation, an agency can use it and impose sanctions on that basis. But against whom, and why? How does an agency assert power?

Jurisdiction is the legal right of an administrative agency. Jurisdiction empowers administrative agencies to hear and decide controversies and to impose sanctions. This is how they assert power.

Jurisdiction in administrative law requires the following:

- **Personal jurisdiction**—authority over parties (including "intervenors"[1]) involved in the proceeding; or
- **Subject-matter jurisdiction**—the power to adjudicate a particular type of matter and provide the remedy demanded[2]; and
- **The agency's scope of authority**—explained in the enabling statute of every individual agency.[3]

Administrative agency tribunals lack subject-matter jurisdiction if they lack the statutory power to consider a matter.[4] As a result, decisions of administrative tribunals are valid only if the tribunals can legally assert jurisdiction.[5]

---

1. Duhaime.org, *Learn Law, Intervener Definition*, www.duhaime.org; http://www.duhaime.org/LegalDictionary/I/Intervener.aspx (last visited September 25, 2017).
2. Cornell Law School, *Subject Matter Jurisdiction*, www.law.cornell.edu; https://www.law.cornell.edu/wex/subject_matter_jurisdiction (last visited September 25, 2017).
3. *Davis v. Chicago Police Bd.*, 268 Ill. App. 3d 851 (1994).
4. *Livingston Manor, Inc. v. Department of Social Services, Div. of Family Services*, 809 S.W.2d 153 (Mo. App. 1991).
5. *Business and Professional People for Public Interest v. Illinois Commerce Comm.*, 136 Ill. 2d 192 (1989).

On this basis, the best challenge to an administrative agency hearing is to attack jurisdiction as faulty. This can be a repetitive motion attacking lack of jurisdiction. A party can renew the motion to dismiss for lack of jurisdiction. Although jurisdictional failure arguments can be made at any stage of the hearing and appellate process, best practice calls for a party to ensure that the objection to alleged jurisdiction over a party is unequivocally on the record. Counsel can offer arguments addressing the coverage of the agency's enabling statute, case law regarding jurisdiction, and references to testimony or evidence already presented at the hearing.

This can be asserted at several points:

- In paperwork filed before the hearing[6]
- During a prehearing conference call (if one is possible)
- In a motion before the administrative bench officer at the start of the hearing
- After the hearing has started and the bench officer has stated all the preliminary matters on the record[7]
- At the start of presentation of evidence
- At the close of the hearing[8]
- In a posthearing briefing
- On appellate review (see the extensive discussion of judicial review in Chapter 4)[9]

Parties wishing to argue jurisdiction in a posthearing briefing must request and receive agreement from the administrative bench officer for a posthearing briefing schedule. The brief should contain general citations to the record (probably a recording transmitted on request vie e-mail with an attached audio file) as well as case law and the agency's enabling statute defining its jurisdiction.

A prehearing conference is a (usually telephonic) discussion before the evidentiary hearing that includes the administrative judge and the parties or their representatives. Some agencies do not use prehearing conferences, so if an important

---

6. This can be asserted in a letter or formal pleading: Courts may exercise general "all-purpose" personal jurisdiction over a party "to hear any and all claims against it" only when the party's connections with the forum state "are so constant and pervasive as to render it essentially at home in the forum State." *Daimler AG v. Bauman*, 134 S. Ct. 746, 751 (2014; internal quote marks and brackets omitted); specific personal jurisdiction satisfies due process if "the defendant's suit-related conduct" creates "a substantial connection with the forum state." *Walden v. Fiore*, 134 S. Ct. 1115, 1119 (2014); *see also, Goodyear Dunlop Tires Operations S.A. v. Brown*, 564 U.S. 915, 919 (2011); *J. McIntyre Machinery Ltd. v. Nicastro*, 564 U.S. 873, 881 (2011).
7. This would be a motion in *limine* (a motion before the presentation of evidence, which presentation of evidence arguably would be a waste of time because the tribunal lacks jurisdiction over either the matter or the participants). Be ready to offer a pocket brief addressing the coverage of the statute authorizing the agency and case law regarding jurisdiction.
8. A final motion at the end of the evidence is a good approach to motion practice.
9. A jurisdiction defense should be raised with the court via a motion to dismiss early in the process (*Hamilton v. Atlas Turner, Inc.*, 197 F.3d 58 (2d Cir. 1999), cert. den., 53 U.S. 1244 (2000)).

> matter (such as a challenge for lack of jurisdiction) needs to be argued, a party can request that the agency schedule one, and explain why.
>
> The moving party should have references ready regarding the agency's enabling statute, the agency's hearing processes, and case law.

If the agency does not use prehearing telephonic conferences, a motion to dismiss for lack of jurisdiction can be offered in other ways before or during the hearing.

If successful, at any stage, this attack on jurisdiction wipes the entire hearing process and any subsequent decisions off the map. It likely stops the clock running, as well, on any timelines related to issues that are part of the matter; be sure to include in your motion a request to rewind all time deadlines if you win. This victory is a complete defense to enforcement or sanctions that the agency alleges are part of the case. It is as if no action had ever been taken.

The same arguments are true regarding challenging decisions of a city council or similar governmental body. If the city charter or municipal code or other laws do not confer power on the governmental body to hear and decide the issue before it, regarding the parties in front of it, no amount of talking can confer jurisdiction.

Jurisdiction is one of the most powerful challenges to administrative actions and one of the most powerful restraints on administrative exercise of power. If jurisdiction in the tribunal is proper, however, the next issue is ways to powerfully and successfully work through the mechanics of the hearing.

Once the agency representative (city attorney, advocate, or other designee) begins to present evidence from the agency's administrative file, counsel can lodge an objection based on jurisdiction to this evidence, as flowing from an agency that took action against a party without jurisdictional authority to do so. Be ready with a pocket brief[10] addressing the coverage of the statute authorizing the agency and case law regarding jurisdiction.

> Most administrative bench officers, before going on the record at the beginning of the hearing, ask whether parties have issues to discuss. This is a time to tell the administrative bench officer that you have what could be a dispositive motion. The administrative bench officer will hear the motion and likely take it under advisement, deferring a ruling until after the hearing, likely well after the close of the record. Be prepared to offer the administrative bench officer a brief, with some case law regarding jurisdiction and referencing the statute under which the agency operates.

---

10. A pocket brief is a short brief that counsel prepares before trial that addresses evidentiary issues that have not already been addressed in Motions in Limine but that counsel expect might come up in trial.

6

Before the Hearing: Preparing to Put on a Case in a Federal or State Administrative Court

General Hearing Procedures

Texas as an Example

Parties in contested cases are entitled to respond to the government's accusations and present evidence and argument at a hearing, after reasonable notice.[1] Parties are entitled to assistance of counsel.[2]

In contested cases, if a majority of agency officials responsible for the final decision have not heard the case or read the record, the final decision may not be rendered until a proposed decision is served on each party. All parties may then file exceptions and submit written legal arguments.[3]

Managing Evidence Issues

Generally, the rules of evidence are not strictly enforced. Hearsay evidence is often admitted into the record (although the agency decision may not rest solely on hearsay). To foster full disclosure of facts, parties may cross-examine witnesses at agency hearings.[4] Evidence that is irrelevant or repetitious is properly excluded.[5]

---

1. See Tex. Gov't. Code § 2001.051.
2. See Tex. Gov't. Code § 2001.053.
3. See Tex. Gov't. Code § 2001.062.
4. See Tex. Gov't. Code § 2001.087.
5. See Tex. Gov't. Code § 2001.082.

Judgments

A final written decision (or decision and order) must either be in writing or stated on the record.[6] It must include explicit findings of fact (evidence in the record) and conclusions of law.

Note
If an agency's regulation, or application of an agency regulation, interferes with or impairs a legal right or privilege of an individual or group, the agency must issue a declaratory judgment with respect to the validity or applicability of a rule.[7]

Individuals or groups who have final decisions from a Texas administrative agency and have exhausted all remedies available through the agency may seek judicial review of the agency's action[8] by filing a petition.[9] Parties may appeal final district court judgments as directed for civil actions generally.[10]

Once rules and regulations are published, heard, reviewed, and approved, they can be used and applied. Most applications of administrative regulations go unnoticed and unremarked-on. But sometimes, they trigger litigation.

When a government agency acts through its sanction power to enforce a regulation, it issues citations or other notice of violation against a member of the public, a business, or other regulated entity. When the cited person or group opposes the sanction but the agency does not cancel the sanction, the next step is usually an adversarial hearing before an administrative bench officer (sometimes called an administrative judge, hearing officer, or hearing examiner). At times, hearings are before governmental councils, rather than administrative bench officers, but this is unusual.

Counsel might need to correct some client misapprehensions regarding administrative agency hearings. Although many members of the public see adversarial proceedings on television (almost all courtroom reality TV shows are actually binding arbitration, a form of administrative proceeding), these portrayals of the administrative hearing process can be misleading for clients who are not lawyers.

To prepare clients for administrative agency hearings, counsel can mention that most administrative bench officers have tremendous respect for the judicial process. They do not want to be on television and do not want to engage in attention-grabbing conduct. Rather, they want to engage in a search for the truth, usually a fairly quiet pursuit.

---

6. See Tex. Gov't. Code § 2001.141.
7. See Tex. Gov't. Code § 2001.038.
8. See Tex. Gov't. Code § 2001.171.
9. See Tex. Gov't. Code § 2001.176.
10. See Tex. Gov't. Code § 2001.901.

Clients might need to hear that most administrative bench officers are not harsh or sarcastic. Parties who make harsh or sarcastic presentations to administrative bench officers might not find a receptive audience. If parties would like to be on the same page as the administrative bench officer, they should try to assist the tribunal in its search for the truth.

Insights for Advocates Facing Administrative Bench Officers

Some agencies have specific guidelines, sometimes called the Bench Officer Bench Book, for their administrative bench officers. These manuals are only guidelines, but most administrative bench officers happily follow them. The manuals are not confidential or otherwise secret.

If counsel expects to practice regularly before a particular agency, or the stakes are particularly high, counsel could benefit from trying to locate the bench book on the Internet. This will help counsel help the tribunal get its job done efficiently, which makes every administrative bench officer happy. It is worth the time it takes to skim the chapters on running a hearing.

Many trial lawyers have experience in civil court. There, the rules of evidence apply, explicit local rules are available for review, and bench officers are well known and frequently discussed (see almost any bar association listserv). Most of this does not apply to administrative proceedings.

Although some skills are transferrable from civil court to an administrative hearing (the ability to ask a question, for example), many new skills are required in an administrative hearing (a somewhat less-regulated proceeding). Counsel should not assume that an administrative hearing is identical to standard civil court proceedings.

Sometimes, administrative bench officers are not well known, so their preferences and quirks are a wild card. Explicit procedural rules may or may not exist; and if they do, they may or may not be findable. If counsel can find them, they may or may not be strictly enforced. The rules of evidence (whether state or federal) more than likely do not apply, or they will be applied unevenly and in unexpected ways.

For example, the Veteran's Administration (VA) has a complicated approval process before advocates may participate in hearings: they must provide information about bar membership, attend fairly extensive training, and receive approval through the VA in Washington, D.C. In other words, most advocates will not be eligible absent an extensive, expensive, lengthy lead-up process. But this also trains counsel regarding the unique burden of proof and assumptions operating in hearings before the VA.

The Social Security Administration (a part of the Department of Health and Human Services) runs hundreds of administrative hearings every day across the

United States. These hearings involve complex medical and scientific testimony, including numerous types of experts. The proceedings include specific emphasis on certain bits of evidence.

Each setting has evolved to include specific rules and expectations. Most of them make a lot of sense for the particular setting. A rich source of reference material is usually available through the agency website and on lawyer group e-mail in the region.

For these and many other reasons, counsel need to conscientiously prepare their cases if they want to capture every possible advantage for their clients' causes. And counsel need to explain this dynamic to clients, so they understand and are prepared for counsel's professional efforts.

Recommendations for Preparing for an Administrative Hearing

Administrative hearings are adversarial proceedings (in this way, similar to trials) and although both are governed by constitutional due process considerations, they differ in procedure and practice. The degree of formality varies widely among various agencies, and approaches to hearing advocacy need to be tailored to the specific demands of the particular tribunal.

The moving party in most administrative agency hearings must present all of the issues, testimony, and documentary evidence necessary to meet any burden of proof. Frequently, in administrative litigation, the burden is on the government to prove the facts underlying its citation action, usually by a preponderance of the evidence, by referencing the facts in the agency's file.

Counsel who pursue careers in administrative advocacy must be prepared to flexibly adjust every presentation to meet the statutory and regulatory standards in the particular case. Agencies set out the particulars in their rules addressing hearings.

The party challenging the agency's proposed action (citation, fine, license review, or other administrative enforcement) should diligently protect and preserve the administrative hearing record. Some agency decisions are ultimately resolved on appeal.

Effective Administrative Advocacy Requires Homework

Try to understand the agency's approach. How did the matter get to this point? Review the enabling statute that creates an agency or vests it with certain powers. The statute may set out some administrative hearing procedures. If they exist and are available, read the agency's procedural regulations, rulings, policy manuals, or internal operating procedures that govern hearings. Sometimes, administrative agency litigation manuals are available online.[11]

---

11. Federal Labor Relations Authority, FLRA litigation manual, www.flra.gov; https://www.flra.gov/system/files/webfm/OGC/Manuals/Litigation%20Manual/Litigation%20Manual_reduced.pdf (last visited September 25, 2017).

If the agency has not adopted procedural rules, review the model rules. The California Office of Administrative Hearings, for example, maintains extensive rules for numerous California administrative hearings that apply to hearings for agencies that do not maintain their own corps of bench officers.[12]

At this time, the federal government is not maintaining a single federal office of administrative hearings. But larger federal agencies maintain their own internal offices of administrative hearings (for example, Immigration and Customs Enforcement). Counsel should check the administrative hearing structure of the applicable agency that is seeking enforcement against counsel's client.

Counsel should read the Federal Administrative Procedure Act[13] or the state or territory's APA. For example, in California, counsel should read the California Administrative Procedure Act;[14] in Texas, check the Texas Administrative Procedure Act.[15] The Florida Administrative Procedure Act is found in Title 10, Part X, Chapter 120 of the Florida Statutes.[16]

Counsel should think about constitutional due process arguments and other procedural requirements that might apply to administrative agencies. Advocates should have a few cases ready to cite if counsel is expecting a challenge or if the advocate wants to assert a challenge.[17]

---

12. California Superior Court, *An Overview of Administrative Hearing Procedure*, www.courts.ca.gov; http://www.courts.ca.gov/partners/documents/2011SRL1eOverview.pdf (last visited September 25, 2017).

13. Cornell Law School, 5 U.S. Code Chapter 5 – Administrative Procedure, www.law.cornell.edu; https://www.law.cornell.edu/uscode/text/5/part-I/chapter-5 (last visited September 25, 2017).

14. California Office of Administrative Law, *Administrative Procedure Act & OAL Regulations*, www.ola.gov.ca; https://oal.ca.gov/publications/administrative_procedure_act (last visited September 25, 2017).

15. Tex. Gov't. Code § 2001.001.

16. https://administrativelaw.uslegal.com/administrative-procedure-acts/florida./.

17. The core of due process is notice and a hearing before an impartial tribunal; rights include discovery and an opportunity to confront (cross-examine). Tribunal decisions must be based solely on evidence in the record; parties must be allowed representation by counsel. Procedural due process protects against improper deprivation of life, liberty, or property. ("[P]rocedural due process rules are shaped by the risk of error inherent in the truth-finding process . . ."; *Carey v. Piphus*, 435 U.S. 247, 259 (1978)); *Mathews v. Eldridge*, 424 U.S. 319, 344 (1976). Due process "minimize[s] substantively unfair or mistaken deprivations" by allowing parties to contest the alleged bases for deprivation of their interests (*Fuentes v. Shevin*, 407 U.S. 67, 81 (1972) (importance of procedural rights and being able to defend one's interests)); *Marshall v. Jerrico, Inc.*, 446 U.S. 238, 242 (1980); *Nelson v. Adams USA, Inc.*, 529 U.S. 460 (2000) (amendment of judgement, imposing attorney fees and costs to sole shareholder of liable corporate structure, held invalid; shareholder was without notice or opportunity to dispute the imposts). Administrative (and executive) proceedings satisfy the due process clause, although not "judicial" (administrative proceedings assessing taxes are not "judicial" proceedings, yet the decisions are enforceable (*McMillen v. Anderson*, 95 U.S. 37, 41 (1877)). Administrative tribunals provide adequate due process: traditional court proceedings are not required (*Ballard v. Hunter*, 204 U.S. 241, 255 (1907); *Palmer v. McMahon*, 133 U.S. 660, 668 (1890)). *De novo* judicial review of the factual bases of state agency decisions is not a requirement of due process (oil field proration order; *Railroad Comm'n v. Rowan & Nichols Oil Co.*, 311 U.S. 570 (1941)). Due process is not denied if judicial review is unavailable; preclusion of judicial review of Veterans Administration decisions regarding veteran's benefits upheld (*Moore v. Johnson*, 582 F.2d 1228, 1232 (9th Cir. 1978). See also, generally, *Griswold v. Connecticut*, 381 U.S. 479 (1965); *Gitlow v. New York*, 268 U.S. 652 (1925); *Lochner v. New York*, 198 U.S. 45 (1905). But no due process violation or bias can be inferred exclusively from an administrative bench officer's adverse credibility determinations of one side's witnesses, evidentiary rulings unfavorable to one side, questioning of one side's witnesses, or alleged expressions of impatience or anger (*United Nurses Association of California v. National Labor Relations Board* (No. 15-70920) (9th Cir. filed Sept. 11, 2017)).

Understand Burden of Proof versus Burden of Persuasion (They Are Not Synonymous)

At an administrative agency hearing, an administrative bench officer reviews the actions of government agencies. Generally, a member of the public or an organization affected by the administrative enforcement action can object to the agency's determination. At this point, the agency offers an internal appellate "paper review" (without a hearing). But eventually an administrative bench officer likely will review the agency's decision through a hearing.

Burden of Proof: Arguing an Agency's Failure or Sufficiency

Burden of proof means a party's duty to persuade the administrative bench officer that the agency's action is either error or largely correct (depends on how the enabling statute allocates the burden). A party does this by offering evidence (of any or all types—testimonial, documentary, demonstrative, or other type) and argument.

Generally, in administrative hearings, the party requesting review before the agency's bench officer does not have the burden of proof (but not always—check the rules). The agency (usually the government, the municipality, or another governmental subdivision) must convince the bench officer of the "rightness" of the agency's position, usually by a preponderance of the evidence.[18] The agency must show that evidence in its file is substantial enough to support the agency's proposed enforcement action.

The party asserting a particular fact generally has the burden of affirmatively proving that fact. This is how the burden of proof falls on the agency, which is technically the appellee, in an enforcement appeal. This is one of the interesting twists of administrative appellate advocacy in agency hearings.

Note

An agency may allocate the burden of proof in an administrative hearing as it pleases, as long as it is not contrary to the agency's enabling statute and is consistent with its overall legislative directive.[19] The agency's rules usually outline the details.

Burden of Persuasion and Standard of Proof: Convincing the Trier of Fact

Standard of proof refers to the degree of evidence or level of evidence required to establish a fact. Preponderance of the evidence is the standard of proof most often found in administrative law (but other standards can be applied; check the underlying, enabling statute for the agency or the regulation you are dealing

---

18. See, generally, *Nassiri v. Chiropractic Physicians' Bd. of Nev.*, 385 P.3d 588 (Nev. 2016).
19. *Bunce v. Secretary of State*, 239 Mich. App. 204 (1999).

with. Also check the regulations themselves, specifically under the heading of Hearings.).

A preponderance of evidence requires that more than 50 percent of the evidence points to the existence or nonexistence of a fact. Sometimes, the phrase "more likely than not" is used interchangeably with "preponderance of the evidence."

Trial Tip

Preponderance of the evidence is judged on the evidence that is more convincing regarding truth or accuracy. It is generally not based on the quantity of evidence. For this reason, an attack on opposing witnesses' credibility at the hearing, usually through a rebuttal case focused on documents, is essential for administrative litigators.

Because appeals rarely disturb credibility findings, a single witness, found credible at the hearing, can overcome quantities of evidence to the contrary.[20]

Standard of Review Considerations

Judicial review is the process by which courts examine the actions of administrative agencies. The standard of review comes into play during this process. The standard of review that courts apply to administrative decisions is informed by the degree of deference given by the court to the agency's action.[21]

After choosing a degree of deference, the court reviews the record for substantial evidence to support the facts the agency is asserting. The court can substitute its own judgment for the agency's determination regarding applying laws, rules, or regulations.

Substantial evidence refers to the quality and quantity of evidence needed to support the agency's factual findings (these findings of fact are the material that support the agency's proposal for enforcement). The analysis of whether substantial evidence exists in the agency's file revolves around whether the agency has provided at the hearing enough information to supports its citation.

The reviewing court then looks at the agency's evidence at the hearing to see whether it was sufficient to support the administrative bench officer's decision to approve or disapprove the agency's proposed enforcement action.

---

20. A single discrepancy in a claimant's testimony is not adequate justification for an administrative bench officer to disregard claimant's testimony in its entirety (*Popa v. Berryhill*, 868 F.3d 764 (9th Cir. 2017), which amended *Popa v. Berryhill*, __ F.3d __, No. 15-16848, 2017 WL 4160041 (9th Cir. Sept. 20, 2017)).
21. The U.S. Supreme Court has set out three degrees of judicial deference: (1) an extremely deferential standard of review under which the reviewing court defers to the agency's interpretations, unless unreasonable (*Chevron U.S.A., Inc. v. NDRC*, 467 U.S. 837 (1984)); (2) the reviewing court defers to the agency's interpretation of its own ambiguous regulations (*Auer v. Robbins*, 519 U.S. 452 (1997)); (3) the reviewing court is not required to defer to the agency's interpretation but gives an appropriate degree of deference, depending on the agency's expertise in the particular matter (*Skidmore v. Swift*, 323 U.S. 134 (1944)).

Understanding Standard of Review

The standard of review for administrative agency decisions means the analysis that a reviewing civil appellate court (a reviewing court is not the administrative tribunal) applies to an agency's decisions (including administrative bench officers' decisions). An agency's proposed enforcement action will be set aside if the proposed action is found to have been arbitrary, abuse of discretion, contrary to law or the Constitution, or in excess of statutory jurisdiction.

The scope of review of facts is usually the substantial evidence test. On questions of law, the court may substitute its judgment for the agency's judgment.[22]

When starting its review analysis, the reviewing court first considers jurisdiction. If jurisdiction is absent, the court ends its review and vacates the action. Assuming that jurisdiction is sound, the court decides which issues before it involve findings of fact versus conclusions of law.

Regarding Questions of Law

To decide questions of law, reviewing courts read and apply the constitutional and statutory clauses that govern the agency. The proper standard of review is the substitution of judgment test; a reviewing court uses its independent judgment to interpret and apply laws and administrative rules and regulations. Reviewing courts do not necessarily defer to the administrative bench officer's analysis regarding interpreting legal questions.

Regarding Questions of Fact

The standard of proof that most commonly applies is substantial evidence.[23] Substantial evidence means that sufficient evidence is in the agency's file so a reasonable person could accept it to support a particular conclusion by an administrative bench officer. An agency action not supported by the facts likely will be struck down.

---

22. Guidelines for this judicial review of federal administrative agency decisions are in the Federal Administrative Procedure Act. State and territorial laws regarding administrative procedures, including review, are usually referred to in their respective APAs.

23. Substantial evidence means "more than a mere scintilla. It means such relevant evidence as a reasonable mind might accept as adequate to support a conclusion." (*Richardson v. Perales*, 402 U.S. 389, 401 (1971); *Landes v. Royal*, 833 F.2d 1365, 1371 (9th Cir. 1987)). Substantial evidence is not synonymous with any evidence. To constitute sufficient substantiality to support the verdict, the evidence must be "reasonable in nature, credible, and of solid value; it must actually be 'substantial' proof of the essentials which the law requires in a particular case." (*Estate of Teed*, 112 Cal. App. 2d 638, 644 (1952); [citations]); *Kruse v. Bank of America*, 202 Cal. App. 3d 38, 51-52 (1988); *Edison Co. v. Labor Board*, 305 U.S. 197, 229 (1938). "While substantial evidence may consist of inferences, such inferences must be 'a product of logic and reason' and 'must rest on the evidence'; inferences that are the result of mere speculation or conjecture cannot support a finding." (*Kuhn v. Department of General Services*, 22 Cal. App. 4th 1627, 1633 (1994)).

Trial Tip

In some states, the burden of producing evidence may shift from one party to an opposing party. In this situation, one party has the burden of going forward with a prima facie, direct case; then the other side must present evidence to rebut the prima facie case that has just been put on.

Even in this situation, however, the burden of persuasion usually rests, ultimately, with the administrative agency or the government (but not always).

Trial Tip

Because the petitioner at the administrative hearing usually must show by a preponderance of the evidence that substantial evidence to support the agency's proposed action is lacking, petitioner's appeal could focus on a lack of substantial evidence in the administrative file.

Areas for counsel's attack would be the incorrect application of the burden of persuasion or a correct application of the incorrect burden of persuasion by the agency or the administrative bench officer, or both.

Remember again that standard of proof is not burden of proof and is not standard of review. These are three different concepts (although they are often discussed in a single, confusing analysis.)

Discovery

Discovery in legal proceedings (including administrative agency hearings) is a formal, and very broad, search for information.[24] The reason for broad discovery is so that all parties will go to trial with as much knowledge as possible. This assists in the search for the truth through the hearing process.

Discovery in administrative hearing advocacy can be either formal or informal efforts (or both) to obtain information from the other side. Discovery is usually completed before trial, but not always. Sometimes, an administrative bench officer will allow (or even request) some discovery activity during the hearing.

Discovery generally includes the following:

- Demands for production of documents from the other side (or sometimes from third parties)
- Depositions of parties and witnesses
- Written interrogatories (written questions and answers provided under oath)

---

24. Law.com, Definition of Discovery, www.dictionary.law.com; http://dictionary.law.com/Default.aspx?selected=530 (last visited September 25, 2017).

- Written requests for admissions of fact
- Examination of the scene(s)

Trial Tip
Before commencing expensive, exhausting formal discovery battles, try first to reach informal agreements regarding cooperating in discovery. Communicate with opposing counsel about documents, admissions, inspections, and other material. Your good-faith, meet-and-confer process, met with noncooperation by the other side, might help the administrative bench officer agree to expand discovery on your request.

If informal discussions are not successful, check the agency's enabling statute and the agency's own rules and regulations to find the limits of discovery (agencies usually allow limited discovery, far less than civil litigators are used to).

Administrative bench officers have discretion to expand discovery, decide how much additional discovery to permit, and determine how much time this can take. Even if not specifically allowed by the statute or the agency's rules, additional discovery can be allowed, at the bench officer's discretion, if not specifically prohibited. If in doubt, make the request.

Requesting Additional Discovery
Parties can request additional discovery in a number of ways: • By letter to opposing counsel and the administrative bench officer • Orally during the prehearing teleconference call with the administrative bench officer and all counsel (if one is available or provided on one side's request) • Orally at any time during the hearing; be ready with a timeframe for completing the additional discovery (if this motion is granted, be prepared with a request to leave the record open for a finite period of time and only for the designated purpose) When asking for additional discovery, address the following: • How it is necessary to the case • How it speaks to a central issue • How it is the least burdensome process available • How it assists in the efficient administration of justice • How it is within the judge's discretion[25]

---

25. See the discussion of application of administrative bench officer discretion at pp. 48, 72, 74, and 127.

Consider third-party subpoenas to witnesses and for records. If met with opposition, not cooperation, in discovery efforts, focus arguments to the administrative bench officer around the following:

- Expense or delay in getting the matter heard
- Whether the discovery tends to support efficient administration of justice
- Whether it promotes the pursuit of the truth

Administrative Discovery and Federal, State, and Territorial Public Records Act Requests

Although discovery in administrative agency proceedings is usually more limited than many civil litigators are used to, some unique, broad areas of discovery are available to parties challenging governmental sanctions assessed through administrative agencies: the federal Freedom of Information Act (FOIA), California Public Records Act (CPRA), Texas Public Information Act (PIA), Florida Sunshine Law (FSL), and other state and territorial government document disclosure laws.[26]

U.S. Territories and Freedom of Information

Puerto Rico

In the U.S. territory of Puerto Rico, the public has a right to government information and public documents under the Puerto Rico Constitution and its civil code, which recognizes citizens' right to inspect and copy "public document[s] of Puerto Rico."[27]

In early 2017, Puerto Rico announced it was planning to draft a FOIA in line with the U.S. federal government's FOIA and U.S. states. The government's concern is that its current FOIA legislation does not include sufficient mechanisms to compel extensive production of records from the government or any subdivision of the government.[28]

As recently as June 2018, a federal district judge in Puerto Rico refused to dismiss a lawsuit that challenged a government board's refusal to comply with public records requests (*Centro de Periodismo Investigativo v. Financial Oversight and Management Board for Puerto Rico*[29]).

---

26. The federal Freedom of Information Act (FOIA) is codified at 5 U.S.C. § 552; the California Public Records Act (CPRA) is codified at Cal. Gov't. Code §§ 6250-6276.48; the Texas Public Information Act is codified at Tex. Gov't. Code §§ 552.001-552.353; the Florida Sunshine Law is codified at Fla. Stat. § 119.01 *et seq.*
27. The public's right of access to government information and public documents is codified at P.R. Laws Ann. Tit. 32, § 1781. *See also, Soto v. Sec'y. of Justice*, 12 P.R. Offic. Trans. 597, 608 (P.R. 1982) (recognizing constitutional right of access to government information).
28. https://thefoiablog.typepad.com/the_foia_blog/2017/01/puerto-rico-to-draft-a-foia-.html.
29. *Centro de Periodismo Investigativo v. Financial Oversight and Management Board for Puerto Rico*, U.S. Dist. Ct. for the Dist. of Puerto Rico (Civil No. 3:17-cv-01743-JAG), relating to the U.S. federal government's recent financial bail-out of the territory of Puerto Rico and the subsequent reorganization of the territory's finances.

Guam

The Guam territorial government and its subdivisions must comply with the Freedom of Information Act (FOIA) or Sunshine Reform Act of 1999 (codified at 5 GCA, Ch. 10). The Guam FOIA provides that every person has the right to inspect and copy any public document on Guam, except as otherwise expressly prohibited.[30]

Other U.S. Territories

Advocates seeking government records in other U.S. territories should check the territorial statutes regarding the extent of cooperation required of government entities. Some useful case law regarding application of the statutory requirements might be available in annotated codes or elsewhere.

The FOIA, CPRA, PIA, FSL, and other state and territorial transparency laws can be used to request documents (but *not* to demand answers to requests for admissions, secure answers to interrogatories, or responses to other traditional discovery options).[31] However, cleverly crafted FOIA, CPRA, PIA, FSL, and other document requests under statutes can provide useful answers, as if to interrogatories or requests for admissions. FOIA, CPRA, PIA, FSL, and other requests can be used instead of, or in conjunction with, other discovery. It is considered a best practice to inform the other side and copy the bench officer on public records requests.

Examples of useful documents that can be requested under FOIA, CPRA, PIA, FSL, and other state and territorial acts include the following:

- Internal memoranda
- Interpretive documents regarding implementing a statute or regulation
- Internal or external e-mails (or both)
- Statistical analyses[32] (governments compile loads of statistics and analyze them at length)

Trial Tip

A request for documents related to cases similar to the case currently in litigation could yield illuminating material. Relevance is not a valid basis to deny counsel's request for documents. Failure or refusal of a government to provide properly requested documents can be a valid basis to postpone the hearing.

---

30. http://www.guamlegislature.com/Public_Laws_25th/P.L.%2025-76.pdf.
31. First Amendment Coalition (FAC), *Public Records – How to Navigate FAC's Public Records Resource;* www .firstamendmentcoalition.org; https://firstamendmentcoalition.org/public-records-2 (last visited September 25, 2017).
32. National Freedom of Information Coalition, *Sample FOIA Request Letters;* www.nfoic.org; http://www.nfoic .org/sample-foia-request-letters (last visited September 25, 2017).

No government administrative agency is under an obligation to create documents in response to counsel's document requests. If no statistical analyses exist that match the requested document description, the agency will not create one. Counsel should make requests narrow enough to describe the information counsel needs, while not so broad as to result in an unintelligible deluge of random data.

Caveat

Don't request thoughtlessly broad document sets from the agency holding your hearing. The same staff working to put your hearing together might also be responding to your public records request. It doesn't help your case to strike the staff as a thoughtless advocate. (To facilitate your document-request efforts, sample FOIA requests, appeals, and requests for fee waiver are online.[33])

As an example of how data requests in an administrative hearing setting can be helpful in both administrative proceedings and in related civil litigation, after a 2018 death from Legionnaires' disease in Southern California, local health officials connected the outbreak to a local amusement park (most of the infected individuals had visited the park). The California Occupational Safety and Health Administration (Cal.-OSHA) is the state administrative agency with jurisdiction over these types of events.

After investigating the outbreak, Cal.-OSHA cited the park for failing to properly clean water-cooling equipment (and related violations). The fine was $33,000. Interestingly, Cal.-OSHA never announced the fine; the information was discovered only through a third party's assertion of legal rights to data disclosure.[34]

Because the death could be tied to the park's failure to properly clean its equipment, Cal.-OSHA's administrative findings and associated fine likely will be cited in civil litigation seeking money damages to compensate the family of the deceased park patron and for the individuals sickened by the park conditions. Because some of the victims were injured while employed by and working at the park, this could trigger Workers' Compensation proceedings, up to and including administrative hearings.

This is an example of how counsel can use information obtained through an administrative process in subsequent civil litigation as well as subsequent administrative proceedings before separate agencies. Counsel's aggressive use of nontraditional discovery tools in administrative litigation settings is one area of excellence

---

33. First Amendment Coalition, *Sample CPRA Request Letter;* www.firstamendmentcoalition.org; https://firstamendmentcoalition.org/public-records-2/sample-cpra-request-letter/ (last visited September 25, 2017). Freedom of Information Foundation of Texas, *TPIA Letter;* www.foift.org; http://foift.org/resources/letter-templates/pia-letter/ (last visited September 25, 2017).
34. https://www.latimes.com/local/california/la-me-ln-legionnaires-disney-20180904-story.html.

in representation that administrative litigators can wield on behalf of their clients, which traditional civil litigators sometimes overlook or fail to use effectively.

Public Records Act requests are generally free, although some copying costs might be assessed—check to see whether you can avoid this by providing "in-package" computer discs with postage-paid padded envelopes or by accepting e-mail transmissions.[35]

Requests for fee waivers can be included with information requests; clients on public assistance usually receive waivers, so public information requests should come from them as individuals and go directly to the agency. Parties with retained counsel rarely secure fee waivers.

Rules of Evidence

Traditional rules of evidence (either federal rules of evidence or local state rules) apply to administrative proceedings only to the extent the administrative bench officer prefers. Constitutional due process requirements, however, are always an important limitation on evidentiary practice. Evidence that reasonably prudent individuals would rely on probably will be admitted.

The hearsay rule applies in administrative tribunals in only a limited fashion: evidence characterized as hearsay is admissible, but it cannot be the sole basis of the administrative bench officer's decision. For this reason, corroborating evidence is needed to shore up the hearsay evidence that a party offers as a basis for a decision by the administrative bench officer. An administrative hearing decision based entirely on hearsay evidence likely will be overturned.

Objections

In advance of the hearing, counsel should try to anticipate possible objections to documents and testimony, and sketch out a few responses. Similarly, counsel should try to anticipate the evidence that opposing counsel likely will introduce, consider bases for objections (if any), and sketch out objections to preserve the record for appeal.

All administrative proceedings are bench proceedings, so the risk of prejudice to the jury is absent. As a result, evidentiary exclusionary rules are generally not strictly applied. Relevance is always a central issue, however, when considering allowing evidence into the record. Counsel should never hold back on relevance arguments, if for no other reason than to preserve the issue in the record.

Other useful objections in administrative proceedings include the following:

- *Leading*—opposing counsel is testifying yet does not have first-hand knowledge of any relevant facts (leading questions are very common in administrative hearings).

---

35. League of California Cities, *A Guide to the California Public Records Act* (Revised April 2017), www.cacities .org; https://www.cacities.org/Resources/Open-Government/THE-PEOPLE%E2%80%99S-BUSINESS-A-Guide-to-the-California-Pu.aspx (last visited September 25, 2017).

- *Calls for speculation*—the question opposing counsel put to the witness does not seek to elicit a personal observation of the witness that is relevant to any aspect of the matter. Rather, it asks the witness to make a guess about something. This is not useful testimony, unless the witness has been properly qualified as an expert.
- *Calls for a narrative answer*—narrative testimony does not answer any particular question and results in a confused (and therefore somewhat useless) record.
- *Asked and answered*—if opposing counsel asks the same question more than once of the same witness, this wastes judicial and agency resources and allows for improper emphasis on selected testimony.
- *Cumulative*—repetitive testimony from different witnesses needlessly clutters and burdens the record but adds nothing new to an understanding of the case.
- *Relevance*—opposing counsel's question calls for testimony that is more of a distracting tangent than testimony on a relevant point.
- *Assumes facts not in evidence*—opposing counsel is asking the witness a question that includes facts to which no witness has yet testified. In this way, opposing counsel (who has no personal knowledge about the facts) tries to insert facts into the record, absent a witness with knowledge to put on the stand (who would then be subject to cross-examination).
- *Lack of personal knowledge*—the witness' testimony is without adequate foundation.
- *Misstatement of the record*—opposing counsel is misquoting a witness.

Mediated Resolution

Settlement discussions can be fact-finding reconnaissance. Listen carefully!

In mediation, the other side often can't help but reveal its litigation strategy and settlement intentions. This information can guide litigation strategy, discovery, witness preparation, and other advocacy tasks.

Trial Tip

If the case doesn't settle during mediation, use the mediator (before everyone leaves the mediation) to help secure stipulations or a joint statement of issues.

Everyone has already cleared the time, left the office, paid for parking, and travelled for the mediation. This can assist the administrative bench officer with the efficient administration of justice, save your client money (always popular), and reduce everyone's stress level.

Note
Negotiated settlements reached before an agency hearing as a result of mediation must be reviewed and approved by the agency itself (authority to commit to settlement terms is never delegated). For this reason, the approval procedure for mediated resolutions can add time to the overall process. Counsel should schedule accordingly.

Research the Presiding Administrative Bench Officer

Inquire whether the administrative bench officer (sometimes referred to as the administrative law judge, hearing examiner, presiding officer, or judge) is employed by the agency or is dispatched from some central Office of Administrative Hearing (or a similar agency).

Try to find decisions by the bench officer to figure out areas of emphasis. Do not skip footnotes to decisions; sometimes, footnotes are where administrative bench officers write freely about their overall approach to the legal analysis.[36]

Use public law and litigation group e-mail to send out feelers for information. Do not overlook government lawyers who regularly appear in administrative settings (city attorneys, federal agency lawyers). On the local bar group e-mail (among other venues), ask about the agency hearing process and the administrative bench officers there.

Ask colleagues who know the administrative bench officer:

- How actively does the administrative bench officer participate in counsel's presentations?
- How does the administrative bench officer treat counsel, clients, and witnesses?
- How does the administrative bench officer like evidence to be marked and submitted?
- How does the administrative bench officer apply the rules of evidence, including handling objections?
- How flexible is the administrative bench officer regarding developments during the hearing?
- What are some of the administrative bench officer's quirks?

Agency decisions from particular bench officers might not be compiled. Sometimes, administrative bench officers do not preside often enough for a body of

---

36. Careful review of footnote language can reveal an administrative judge's overall approach to administrative jurisprudence. This can be invaluable when preparing for your next hearing.

jurisprudential evidence to exist. If so, there's no need for concern; this means that the agency cannot count on the administrative bench officer to decide in a particular direction, either.

Facilities Concerns

Administrative hearings are held in fancy courtrooms, municipal hearing rooms, stuffy conference rooms, and supply closets. The pursuit of justice needs constitutionally sound jurisdiction and due process. The details of the environment are just details—counsel should not become distracted.

Counsel should try to visit the hearing venue before the scheduled hearing date to observe a prior hearing. Counsel can get an idea of the experience and share this information with clients and witnesses (and perhaps discuss obvious difficulties with opposing counsel) as part of counsel's hearing prep. Everyone involved needs to understand that hearing rooms regularly get moved or switched at the last minute.

Almost all hearings are open proceedings. Often, executives from the agency sit in to observe for various reasons and members of the general public drop by. Strangers to the proceeding wander in because they are lost. Security might also poke a head in.

On a sound basis, the administrative bench officer might be convinced to close the hearing to protect minors, preserve financial privacy, or another compelling reason. Witnesses may be sequestered (excluded), as in standard civil trials. If counsel can articulate good cause, counsel should not hesitate to make the request.

Trial Tip

Discuss with the administrative bench officer's staff the facilities for displaying graphic evidence: computer and monitor on a rolling cart, ELMO projector and screen, large-format paper pad or chalkboard on an easel, anything needed for demonstrations (usually, nothing at all is provided for counsel—everything must be brought in and then correspondingly removed).

You must bring absolutely everything with you to display graphic evidence and facilitate use of courtroom technology. You will need to set up whatever is needed before the start of the hearing, including easels, projectors, and monitors.

Remember to bring any of the following you might need:

- Extension cords and power cords
- Connectors and cube taps (multiplugs)
- Markers (various colors)
- A contingency back-up, in case of technology failure (which happens more often than you might expect)
- Anything else you can think of

Counsel should determine how the record is going to be preserved; discuss with the client purchasing a copy of the transcript, if one can be prepared. If appeal is a possibility, and the agency does not provide court reporting, one party might have to pay a court reporter. Make advance arrangements accordingly.

Once the evidence, witnesses, and technology are in order, the next step is live advocacy before the administrative tribunal. Although some individuals get anxious before the hearing, most hearings are fairly informal.

Anyone can ask for a break at any time; the administrative bench officer is not trying to make the process painful. Although it is a mistake to treat the process lightly, neither should anyone lose sleep over these proceedings.

Use of Exhibits and Managing Evidence

Some administrative agency rules include protocols for submitting documentary evidence and may even prescribe exhibit numbering or formatting standards, so make sure to check this and comply. Before the hearing, prepare an index of the evidence counsel might need or want to get into the record, as well as a binder with numbered exhibits: check off each item as it is admitted (see Appendix A, Index of Exhibits for an example).

Depending on the type of case, submitting exhibits to the presiding administrative bench officer before the hearing, before going on the record, may be preferable. Ask the administrative bench officer and confer with opposing counsel to work this out as early as possible in the process.

The procedure for introducing exhibits at an administrative hearing is less formal than in standard civil trial proceedings, but counsel should be prepared to lay a sufficient foundation concerning the following:

- Who is vouching for the exhibit under oath?
- Why was the exhibit prepared?
- When was the exhibit prepared?
- How was the exhibit prepared?
- Where was the exhibit found?
- What hearsay exceptions might be needed?

Admitting all documents and other evidence before going on the record may work well if the parties are merely stipulating to the admissibility of unobjectionable documents. Be sure, however, that objections to the admissibility of a document take place on the record.

Counsel should ensure that the way exhibits come into evidence highlights for the administrative bench officer (and any appellate tribunal) the purpose, authenticity, and reliability of the exhibit.

7

During the Hearing: Mastering the Administrative Hearing Process

Crafting Your Opening Statement

Before going on the record, counsel should request the administrative bench officer's permission to make an opening statement. Counsel should not be surprised if the request is denied; it happens. If so, counsel can ask permission of the administrative bench officer to submit an opening statement in writing; counsel should ask to keep the record open for a definite period of time (14 days, for example) for this purpose.

Many administrative bench officers begin the hearing with a boilerplate introduction describing the basic process. They then move into particular areas of preliminary inquiry based on their review of the file.

Once the proceeding has officially started and is on the record, the agency attorney (federal agency attorney, city attorney, county attorney, judge advocate general (JAG) officer, assistant U.S. attorney, state assistant attorney general, or even a certified third-year law student) generally has the burden of proof (sometimes the petitioner/appellant may have the burden of proof, but this is unusual) and makes the first opening statement. The administrative bench officer is expecting and listening for opening statements at this stage, so counsel should not reserve for later (unless the administrative judge has denied counsel's request for an opening statement). Counsel should open strong.

Counsel should use lists to address multiple issues; work from bullet points. Reading an opening statement from a prepared script drains the urgency from the presentation. Counsel should resist the temptation to over-prepare and then read word for word. Counsel will become a more skilled advocate by detaching from the prepared script. This is a skill worth practicing to achieve mastery.

Counsel should tally the evidence that supports the client's position, while working from the bulleted list. Counsel should remember to speak slowly—the administrative bench officer will be taking notes and counsel is making important points. It is also important to be brief.

To end strongly, counsel should articulate a "focused ask" regarding the desired remedy. This is critically important. Without a clearly articulated remedy requested on the record at the start of the proceeding, a party can win in the proceeding but, surprisingly, still lose the matter on the remedy.

Example
Client is cited for two code violations and fined. Fines are multiplying as time progresses, and they have been transferred to the tax rolls. As a result, failure to pay triggers a tax lien on the client's home.
After a hearing, the administrative bench officer issues a decision and order overturning one alleged code violation and cancelling the fines related to that alleged violation. This does not remove the fines related to the other code enforcement citation, which remains as a tax lien, albeit a somewhat smaller one. The client's home is still in danger, despite the win. This can occur absent a clearly articulated request to remove the entire tax lien on the property.

The Judge's Role in Direct Examination

Administrative bench officers frequently question parties or witnesses directly. Sometimes (especially when one side is not represented by counsel), the administrative bench officer will question parties and witnesses to ensure due process and meet other constitutional requirements. After the administrative bench officer is done with these inquiries, counsel can solicit further testimony, as needed.[1] Counsel should not be thrown off his or her presentation if the administrative bench officer questions the client. The administrative bench officer will likely revert to a more neutral stance once the questioning is over.

Counsel should listen carefully to the administrative bench officer's direct questioning (of both witnesses and counsel) and take careful notes. This is a guide to the officer's thought processes and is valuable in shaping the rest of counsel's advocacy on the file. This can be a roadmap to closing argument and a posthearing briefing.

---

1. If the administrative bench officer outright precludes further questioning of the witness by counsel, this could be a constitutional due process objection that might be successful on appeal. Make sure to note the objection on the record.

Trial Tip

You can ask the administrative bench officer on the record if he or she is concerned about a particular point or issue. This colloquy is too valuable to forgo, no matter how awkward the exchange may feel.

One of your most important jobs as an advocate at the hearing is to assist the administrative bench officer in the pursuit of the truth. A respectful inquiry can help counsel help the administrative bench officer sort through the case.

Smoothly inviting this on-the-record colloquy with the bench officer showcases is the type of skill and confidence that elevates you to experienced status and generates respect within the legal industry.

CAVEAT

Make objections sparingly, as needed to make a record for appeal. Sometimes, you can offer to set up a continuing projection, with a clearly stated beginning, end, and testimonial subject matter. As an alternative to objecting on every item, make notes of hearsay, relevance, and testimonial weaknesses. Focus on them in closing argument and posthearing briefs.

Trial Tip

If the administrative bench officer overrules your evidentiary objections, offer to submit a posthearing brief to preserve the issue for appeal. You risk alienating the administrative bench officer if you argue at the hearing.

Objections to the administrative bench officer's questioning of a party or witness who is in the witness box on direct examination is a controversial advocacy practice. Listening for and analyzing the subtle messages coming from the administrative bench officer is too valuable to lose with an ill-timed objection.

A better practice is to listen carefully to the administrative bench officer's line of inquiry. If necessary, counsel can make an objection at the end of the bench officer's questioning of the witness, with a clear reference on the record to the start and end of the objectionable queries.

Trial Tip

Before objecting to a judge's question of a witness, be sure the question and answer set has hurt your case. If no real damage has been done to the case, graciously move on.

> ### Trial Tip
>
> Sometimes, an administrative bench officer seems to be obviously favoring the other side. Do not panic over this. This technique sometimes subtly indicates that the seemingly favored side has glaring weaknesses in its case.
>
> Ask the administrative bench officer if the court would like to hear from any additional witnesses from your side or review any additional documentary evidence from your side. Most likely, the administrative bench officer will punt the question back to you, further sharpening the contrast between intense direct questioning of the other side and a hands-off approach to your side.

Advocacy Before Panels of Multiple Administrative Bench Officers

Many state and federal agencies and private arbitration tribunals use multiple hearing officers, working on panels, to hear and decide cases. This is a somewhat controversial practice.

Under many circumstances, counsel and client will be forced to wait to be heard while the scheduling authority tries to coordinate the schedules of multiple busy administrative bench officers, then get dates that work for private counsel. On the other end of the process, the eventual decision will lag and, when it eventually is issued, it will sound like it was written by a camel (because it was written by committee; the most junior hearing officer probably did a pretty good draft that was mostly ready for finalization. But the other two authors inserted jarring commentary in a variety of writing styles. So, if you have trouble following some of the analyses? Not your fault.)

A hearing with multiple administrative bench officers brings a unique set of challenges for advocates. Counsel is certainly trying to follow the leads of the administrative bench officers regarding their areas of concern. Advocates are adjusting their presentation in response to cues from the bench. But counsel should know that the bench officers might have taken a few minutes to discuss the status of the file before taking the bench. They might be aware of each other's areas of concern and have an interest in making sure that these areas of concern are addressed at the hearing. As a result, administrative bench officers frequently ask questions of the advocates on behalf of one of the other members of the panel. This can be confusing if counsel is trying to decode each officer's areas of interest and adjust the presentation accordingly.

Instead of getting tied in a knot, counsel should remember that all bench officers are measuring the evidence against the requirements of the controlling statutes and applying the burden of proof. So long as counsel hews to the applicable statutes and marshals the evidence for some organized advocacy in closing arguments or posthearing briefs, counsel has a strong chance of leading the bench officers through an organized analysis that they will repeat during deliberations.

In this way, counsel might be able to continue to influence the outcome even after the matter is taken under submission.

The Prima Facie Case and Direct Examination by the Government Lawyer

Direct examination is designed to establish a prima facie case. For this reason, all basic factual and legal requirements must be addressed. This is the basis for a sound record at the administrative agency tribunal stage that can support a successful appeal by the agency, if necessary.

Trial Tip
Sometimes, stipulations of the parties can short-cut direct examination, in whole or in part. Many administrative agency hearings are focused more on the interpretation and meaning of the facts than on credibility conflicts regarding what the facts actually are.

Start and end witness testimony on strong points; crisply address weak points in the middle of direct exam. Keep a brisk pace throughout.

Present facts showing how general concepts of fairness favor your side at the end of the direct testimony by witnesses.[2] Administrative proceedings never have juries present, and administrative bench officers are generally resistant to obvious emotional manipulation.

Counsel should work with witnesses to avoid narrative testimony. Narrative testimony is a witness relating information as a story, instead of offering a clear and specific answer to a clear and specific question. The problem with narrative testimony is that no questions are being asked, so no objections can be lodged, and improper evidence comes in.

Trial Tip
You should prepare witnesses so they learn to wait for a question from you, then answer it, and then stop talking. It is awkward, but it is mandatory.

Although the rules of evidence do not apply to administrative tribunal proceedings, the record nevertheless needs to be reasonable clear. Narrative testimony is the opposite of this.

---

2. In this type of context, equity usually means fairness.

An effective method to avoid narration and bring out important evidence through a witness is for counsel to peg the question-and-answer sets with the witness to the documents counsel is offering into the record.[3]

Trial Tip
Do not over-prepare witnesses. They need to speak their own truths in their own ways to be persuasive. Appropriate hearing preparation of witnesses focuses more on helping them focus their answers and get comfortable with the question-and-answer format on the stand, rather than on providing counsel's preferred answers (a fine, but important, distinction).   When witnesses sound like lawyers, listeners lose interest.

Short speaking objections are usually allowed in administrative tribunals (objection, leading; objection, hearsay; objection, assumes facts not in evidence). Counsel should remember to always protect the record of the proceeding, with an eye toward possible appeal. This is not the time to be shy.

Keep an eye on the administrative bench officer's demeanor. Is the bench officer struggling to understand the testimony? If so, counsel should address the problem in real time. Is an unfamiliar accent the problem? Is the witness speaking too quickly or too softly? Are the acoustics in the room poor?

Counsel should ask for direction on how to facilitate the administrative bench officer's understanding of this testimony. Counsel can work to adjust the questioning or otherwise address the barrier to the administrative bench officer's understanding. Witnesses might need to switch locations, speak up, slow down, get closer to the microphone, or some other accommodation.

Trial Tip
Live testimony, with cross-examination, is your most powerful tool in an administrative hearing. But some witnesses just cannot testify (illness, incarceration, outside of the jurisdiction, conflicting subpoena to appear at a higher-level court on the same day, or other understandable reason.)   Administrative bench officers sometimes accept sworn declarations or affidavits in place of live testimony.[4] In these situations, notify the administrative bench

---

3. Counsel should have already asked the administrative bench officer if it is desirable to move all the documents into the record at the end of the case, or some other method (this is also the conversation in which counsel can confirm how they would like submitted evidence marked and identified: letters and numbers? numbers only? something else?).

4. A witness declaration is a written statement, signed under penalty of perjury, which recites facts within the personal knowledge of the person signing (the declarant) that relate to a legal proceeding (including administrative hearings). An affidavit is similar to a declaration, but affidavits are signed under oath before a notary public or

officer's staff that sworn written testimony will be submitted, and explain why.[5] Although the declaration or affidavit's contents are arguably hearsay, hearsay testimony is usually allowed in administrative hearings. In addition, because no jury is present in an administrative tribunal, testimony by sworn written document is almost as effective as live testimony for a bench officer (cross-examination is limited, so the testimony is not tested through confrontation). As well, a subpoenaed witness with live testimony challenges can take the stand and testify from the witness's own prior declaration or affidavit, if necessary.

Once the direct case is done, the other side has a chance to cross-examine. In administrative proceedings, where discovery is limited, cross-examination can be pivotal to the outcome.

Caveat

Avoid judgmental statements during the witness' testimony. Instead, take good notes for later use. The time to comment on credibility and the weight to accord the testimony is during closing argument.

The party challenging the government enforcement action has an opportunity to put on a direct case after the government rests (assuming the government has the burden, which is usually the case). The party appealing the government citation or enforcement action generally does not have the burden of proof. In reality, however, the party challenging the government needs to show in its direct examination that the record does not include substantial evidence to support the agency's citation.

Although most counsel understand the difficulty of proving a negative (in other words, the absence of adequate data in the file), because administrative hearings revolve exclusively around the contents of the agency's file at the time the decision to issue the citation was made, proving insufficient evidence is not as difficult as would normally be expected. Counsel need only work through the written material regarding the client and apply the municipal code, city charter, and agency

---

other official. Because both documents are signed under penalty of perjury under the laws of the relevant jurisdiction, both are usually accepted as substitutes for live testimony.

5. Assuming that no depositions have been taken, and no prior sworn testimony is available, a signed, sworn declaration or affidavit is a good choice. In a declaration or affidavit, the signer (the declarant or affiant) swears or affirms (under the laws of the state in which the affidavit was made as well as the laws of the state where the writing is being offered into evidence (if different)—this is important!—that the statements in the declaration or affidavit, to the best of the witness's knowledge, are true. If the document is not sworn under the laws of the state where the document is being offered, the court might hesitate to accept it. If the document was signed in another state but not sworn to under that state's laws, opposing counsel could object on that basis.

rules to that closed universe of facts. If it makes sense, counsel can call agency employees on the direct case, assuming that the testimony on the agency's direct case is too limited to get at what counsel needs to elicit.

Direct Examination and the Burden of Proof

Counsel for the party suffering the agency's enforcement penalties follows standard guidelines for direct examination. Evidence must be gathered and marked in accord with agency rules, if any. If none exist, counsel can contact opposing counsel to work this out, contact the hearing staff for help, or take other action that makes it easy for the administrative bench officer to work with the evidence both at the hearing and after the hearing when writing the decision and order.

Counsel needs to prepare an organized opening statement. The client must be guided to focus the testimony on the important material, including familiarity with all the documents in the case (from both sides). Clients need assistance mastering the question-and-answer format.

Counsel should pull all the material together in a notebook, including lists to track evidence, objections. Both of these provide structure for closing argument (sample forms are at Appendix A). Notes regarding challenges expected from opposing counsel and ammunition to refute them are useful.

In general, counsel representing parties on the receiving end of government administrative enforcement make the most progress for their clients through cross-examination of the agency's witnesses.

Preparing and Executing Effective Cross-Examination

Discovery in many administrative settings is limited (by law, budget, time, or some combination). As a result, quite often, no prior testimony of the witness is available to provide fodder for cross-examination.

Taking a witness on cross-examination under these circumstances is sometimes called blind cross-examination (or cross-examination by ambush). Because so little formal discovery is available, blind cross at an administrative tribunal requires a different approach than most civil trial advocates are used to. This is the basis for drafting a rough guess about what cross-examination might be like for witnesses on the direct case, as well as preparing witnesses for cross accordingly.

In addition, the rules of evidence are not generally applied in administrative hearings. Hearsay evidence is routinely admitted, so declarants are, functionally, not always present to be cross-examined.

Based on counsel's understanding of the other side's theory of the case, counsel can draft a rough cross-examination for opposing witnesses. This can be supplemented as the witness testifies on direct (see Appendix A, Administrative Hearing Cross-Examination Form).

Effective blind cross-examination calls for a focus different from traditional civil trial cross-examination. Effective administrative litigators think like opposing counsel. To understand the opposing theory of the case, they focus on the few statements and documents provided by the other side. They adjust their cross-examination technique to achieve the following:

- Consider the other side's purpose in calling the witness
- Keep the overall examination short and tailored
- Focus each question on just one single point
- Define the goal(s) for cross-examining each witness—is it admitting important facts? Casting doubt on important facts? Undermining credibility?

Administrative hearings are (usually) tremendously document-centric. Generally, agency counsel tell the client's story through the documentary exhibits. With documents, advocates have powerful tools to control witnesses on blind cross-examination.

Through written exhibits (especially e-mail), advocates can get the opposing witness' own written words into evidence. These real-time documents reflect the unfiltered status quo at the moment of creation, so administrative bench officers place great trust in them. For this reason, effective administrative advocates bear down on e-mails on cross-examination. Sometimes, these print-outs are as good as a deposition, but without the attorney time and client expense.

Once the government witness on the stand reads the contents of the e-mail, counsel can ask whether the witness believed the statement to be a true statement at the time. This can demonstrate that the witness's position changed dramatically in anticipation of trial; if so, counsel likely will be allowed to inquire into whether the witness is concerned about his or her continued employment (or perhaps that this hostile witness actually supports the opposing side's position).

Effective blind cross-examination can be accomplished with an attack on the other side's contention of facts, using focused queries, along the following lines:

- Lead the witness with questions that require short "Yes"/"No" answers, book-ended with "Isn't it true that . . .?," "Wouldn't you agree that . . .?"
- Ask a series of seemingly harmless questions of little importance, in response to which the witness is comfortable agreeing, all of which lead to inevitable agreement on the last, big, important fact.

If a witness manages to do some damage on cross-examination, do not react, and move smoothly but determinedly to the next question.

Trial Tip
Approaching opposing witnesses with business-like respect might get some cooperative answers on cross-examination. But if it does not, do not fall into the hole that the fire-breathing witness is digging.
The more harsh and defensive an opposing witness gets on cross-examination, the less hard you should become on cross-examination. The witness will be less believable with each answer: just keep moving through the question set.
You should relentlessly highlight in closing argument and posthearing briefing the witness' inappropriate demeanor on the stand.

Considering opposing counsel's probable theory of the case, advocates can prepare cross-examination questions for each opposition witness. In administrative proceedings, this usually covers many documents and activities that were well documented. Direct credibility conflicts do arise occasionally but tend to be rare.

Cross-examination should focus on the limits on the agency's actions under the statute that created it and that set out its functions and authority, as well as cutting the alleged connection between what the agency did and the limits of its authority. Lack of substantial evidence in the agency's file to support its action at the time it was authorized is the ultimate showing the administrative bench officer needs to see.

Guidelines for Cross-Examination of Administrative Agency's Expert Witness

Agencies often call experts as witnesses for administrative hearings. This makes sense: the agency employs numerous specially educated and certified specialists as a matter of routine functioning. All of these individuals can realistically be qualified as experts within their areas of function at the agency. As a result, agency counsel have unlimited access to a tailored list of directly relevant expert witnesses, all of whom work in the same building, none of whom can turn down the request to testify, most of whom have administrative courtroom experience. Based on budget and subject-matter limitations, counsel who are opposing agency enforcement actions sometimes have fewer (or no) experts. As a result, administrative hearing advocates who do not work for a government need to make substantial persuasive progress through cross-examination. For this reason, administrative bench officers often allow wide latitude for counsel on cross-examination.

Sometimes, newer advocates have trouble getting started with cross-examination preparation. The following cross-examination structure is a general guide to get administrative counsel warmed up. Counsel should adapt as needed by the particular facts of the case and the type and testimony of the expert.

Attacking the Expert's Qualifications
- You haven't earned the [particular credential, degree, certificate], have you?
- You failed [particular professional testing] the first [numeral] times you attempted it, didn't you?
- You have never published in a peer-reviewed journal in your field, have you? (or have only published a long time ago, or have published very sporadically)
- You have never been invited to publicly present on this topic, have you? (or it was a long time ago, or only sporadically)
- You currently hold zero academic appointments, isn't that correct?
- You have won zero awards in your field, correct? (or too long ago to be currently relevant as the industry has progressed)

Attacking the Expert's Credibility (if research supports these queries):
- Your professional license was [suspended, restricted] by the state licensing board in [year(s)], correct?
- You were convicted of fraud in [year(s)], weren't you?
- You were disciplined in [year(s)] by [relevant professional organization] for [some misconduct], isn't that true?
- In [name of prior matter], didn't the judge find your testimony [unpersuasive, unreliable, unbelievable, untrustworthy]?
- You are currently employed by [name of municipality], correct?
- Your [supervisor, manager, department head] is present in this courtroom [or is expected to review the transcript, if not present], isn't that true?
- It would be natural for an employee to fear for his (or her) future employment in this situation, wouldn't it? (the expert might answer with "I don't know," "No," or "Yes": any answer by the expert is unnecessary because counsel's question says it all).
- If the other side objects, counsel can restate the question as, "Does the presence of your [superior] affect your testimony here today? (If this brings on another objection by opposing counsel, move on. Anything further likely will trigger a migraine in the administrative bench officer, which does not favor your client.)

Attacking Expert Testimony on Insufficient Investigation and Research
- You have a considerable inventory of files for which you are responsible, don't you? How many?
- Considering your responsibilities on all of these files, you didn't have all the time you needed to do a fully complete job in this case, isn't that true? (Expert might answer "Yes" or "No," but it doesn't matter; the question says it all.)
- If the expert says, "No, I had all the time I needed," counsel can ask, "If you had more time on this file, would you have done a better job?" (If the expert says "Yes," counsel can argue later that even the expert believes he or

she could have done a better job; counsel can ask what further activity the expert would have taken on the file, if more time were available.)

- You never reviewed [particular research source or particular document] before preparing your comments on this file, did you?
- When you visited the scene, you didn't bring [particular measuring or study equipment] with you, isn't that true?
- When you visited the scene, you merely viewed the area from a distance, correct?
- You never personally walked around in the [relevant] area, did you?
- You never read [other individual]'s report, did you?
- You never were provided with [particular document or report], were you?
- You never requested to do [particular testing or analyses], did you?
- Through your years of employment with [name of municipality], you have detected some malfunctions in the [testing system, computer system] you used in this case, haven't you?
- Your opinion is based on some number of assumptions, isn't that right?
- You cherry-picked only the supportive facts from the file for today's testimony, didn't you?

Attacking Expert's Testing
- There are other tests you could have performed, correct?
- Is [particular test protocol] one of the tests you could have performed?
- You never performed [particular test], did you?

Attacking the Methodology Underlying Expert's Conclusions
- Your theory in this case was developed for the purpose of trial testimony, correct?
- Your methodology is not generally accepted in the field of [area of study], isn't that true?
- You never [identified, calculated] a margin of error, isn't that right?
- Your methodology in this case has never been peer-reviewed, correct?
- When formulating your analysis in this case, you never ruled out [particular alternative explanation], did you?
- Your analysis in this case doesn't comply with [particular professional standard] does it?

Attacking Expert's Written Findings
- Your reports from other cases are in many ways identical to your report in the case, aren't they?
- You weren't under oath when you wrote [the report, the file notes], were you?

Challenging the Expert Witness Through Learned Treatises
(useful when only one side has an expert)

- Are you familiar with [name of learned treatise] written by [name of author]?
- [Author] is a senior professor of [subject matter] at [institution], correct?
- [Author] has earned a doctorate in [subject matter], are you aware of that?
- Do you consider [author's name]'s volume on [name of treatise or treatise topic] to be authoritative in the area of [restate the designated area of expertise for the expert on the stand]?
- Do you agree [or disagree] with [name of author]'s statement from [name of learned treatise] regarding [causation, or other important scientific or particular area]?

Trial Tip

Opposing witnesses most likely have been prepared to testify at the administrative hearing in chronological order.

If you want the witness to blurt out information in an uncontrolled manner, consider crafting cross-examination questions that work in reverse-chronological order, or start in the middle, or jump around the timeframe.

Caveat

A disrespectful witness will try to bait and argue with you. Arguing with a witness means the advocate has lost control and the witness is running your cross-examination. Do not argue with a witness. Use the inappropriate colloquy to zero in on possible explanations for the witness' bad behavior.

Ask on cross-examination whether the witness is under pressure to shade testimony to support the agency that employs the witness. Ask whether the witness is concerned about adverse job action if he or she does not testify the way the agency employer wants the facts to come out in the hearing.

When Not to Cross-Examine

After listening to the direct examination of the witness, counsel can then decide whether to engage in cross-examination:

- Consider the overall strength of the case. If it is strong, skipping cross-examination minimizes risk.
- Did the direct testimony put a dent in an essential element of the client's case? If not, counsel should not waste time with cross-examination.

- Was the witness inherently unbelievable, whether because of internal contradictions, memory failures, obvious bias, or other apparent problems? If so, there is no need for a lengthy cross-examination of the witness.
- If the witness was expected to but did not bring up damaging testimony on direct, cross-examination might just provide an opportunity to raise the damaging testimony when opposing counsel takes the witness back on redirect examination. Consider skipping cross-examination in this situation.
- If it is important to cross-examine, counsel should consider a narrowly focused cross-examination, to preserve an objection of "outside the scope." But, in reality, almost all administrative bench officers will listen to the redirect, even if "outside the scope."
- If the administrative bench officer sustains the scope objection and excludes the testimony, counsel should beware of the witness being called back on the other side's fake rebuttal case. Unless the other side's proposed rebuttal testimony explains, refutes, or counteracts evidence introduced in counsel's case-in-chief, it is not truly rebuttal evidence; it should be excluded. Even if counsel does not prevail on this objection, there is value in having the objections on the record (appeal, future hearings, posthearing briefs).

Rebuttal Evidence: Traps and Tips

By the time rebuttal evidence is offered, everyone is fatigued. This is the time for counsel to bear down:

- Counsel can object to the fake rebuttal, stating for the record that the proposed rebuttal evidence does not explain, refute, or counteract testimony from the other side.
- Counsel can argue that this testimony is properly part of the other side's case-in-chief, which is long over.
- If the administrative bench officer doesn't suggest it, counsel can ask whether, instead of bringing in actual testimony on rebuttal, the other side can just make an offer of proof[6] (offers of proof are part of the trial record, and can preserve an objection on the record for appeal, but are not themselves testimony or evidence). If so, this is further opportunity for counsel to argue that this evidence is not rebutting anything; it is not explaining, refuting, or counteracting opposing evidence.

---

6. An offer of proof at trial is an advocate's explanation directly to a bench officer explaining how a proposed line of testimony is relevant and admissible. Witnesses do not usually testify as part of a party's offer of proof.

- Counsel can argue that "this exercise is a waste of judicial resources" and "this evidence is needlessly cluttering and burdening the record." These phrases are "dog-whistle"[7] words for the administrative bench officer.

Most likely, objecting counsel will lose this objection. The administrative bench officer probably will allow opposing counsel's fake rebuttal testimony, then allow counsel to cross-examine the opposing witness about it.

But the small victory here is that the administrative bench officer sees an aggressive, clever advocate, not a doormat; opposing counsel is surprised and depleted and will think twice before trying anything shady for the remainder of both advocates' careers; and the record is covered in counsel's objections, preserving them for appeal, if necessary.

Trial Tip
The mark of an effective advocate is knowing when not to speak. Do not feel compelled to talk your way through every possible situation out of a misplaced fear that you are dropping the ball if you sit down and shut up.   Keep the best interests of the client front and center.

Redirect Examination

Redirect examination is usually allowed in administrative proceedings. Similar to standard civil litigation, it is sometimes limited to nonleading questions regarding only topics raised on cross-examination. Many administrative bench officers are fairly loose about this and allow a few rounds of redirect and recross.

Redirect examination clears up confusion regarding key issues. Used incorrectly, however, it reopens disadvantageous areas of questioning, wastes time, and frustrates the administrative bench officer. Effective redirect is brief and covers three or four key topics, at most.

To decide whether to redirect a witness and to focus the questions on this examination, counsel can consider which important facts needed to be established through each witness and notes from cross-examination testimony referencing topics calling for clarifying questions.

Counsel can ask the administrative bench officer for permission to redirect-examine the witness after cross-examination. Advocates can start each area of inquiry on redirect by asking whether the witness recalls answering a specific

---

7. Dog-whistle words are expressions that are loaded with subtle meaning that is understood by only a limited group (in this case, administrative bench officers).

question on cross-examination. Then counsel can pursue the redirect examination line of questioning. This will help orient the administrative bench officer and can get some favorable rulings when the other side objects.

Caveat
Do not withhold important testimony on direct examination, hoping to deploy it to great effect on redirect. Redirect should be limited to rehabilitating the witness' testimony and is at the discretion of the administrative bench officer. The rules in administrative hearings are so flexible that an advocate can't know with certainty whether redirect will even be permitted; if not, the powerful testimony could be lost forever. It is not worth the risk.

Rebuttal and Surrebuttal

Rebuttal (and surrebuttal[8] [advocacy responding to rebuttal to the initial proposition]) testimony is offered to explain, repel, counteract, or disprove evidence presented by an adverse party.[9] Rebuttal evidence disproves points first presented at the trial in the case-in-chief of the opposing party.[10] It cannot be used to clarify prior testimony.

Testimony may not be offered only as additional support to an argument made in a case-in-chief. If the testimony is not solicited "to contradict, impeach or defuse the impact of the evidence offered by an adverse party," it is improper on rebuttal.[11]

The basic guidelines for admission of rebuttal (or surrebuttal) evidence are that

- it need not be based on surprise. Rebuttal evidence may be used to contradict evidence that could reasonably have been anticipated.
- the purpose of rebuttal evidence is to respond to new points or new evidence first introduced by the opposing party, not just to contradict or corroborate evidence already presented.
- rebuttal should not be used as a tool to withhold pieces of the case-in-chief, thus denying the defense a chance to respond in its case-in-chief.

Almost any competent evidence is admissible in rebuttal, if the evidence is appropriate under the circumstances. For example, hearsay evidence was allowed

---

8. Merriam-Webster, definition of surrebuttal, www.merriam-webster.com; https://www.merriam-webster.com/legal/surrebuttal (last visited September 25, 2017).
9. *Sterkel v. Fruehauf Corp.*, 975 F.2d 528, 532 (8th Cir. 1992).
10. *Bean v. Riddle*, 423 S.W. 2d 709 (Mo. 1968).
11. *Peals v. Terre Haute Police Dep't*, 535 F.3d 621, 628 (7th Cir. 2001) (quoting *United States v. Grintjes*, 237 F.3d 876, 879 (7th Cir. 2001).

to rebut the defendant's evidence that a police informant's testimony had been coerced.[12] Rebuttal evidence, if otherwise proper for rebuttal, should be permitted even if it could have been presented as part of the case-in-chief.[13]

Once questioning of witnesses is completed, the administrative bench officer likely will allow a few minutes off the record to regroup and prepare for closing arguments or discussions of briefing schedules, or the like. Witnesses can go home; technology can be broken down and packed up.

Closing Argument

The purpose of closing argument in an administrative hearing is to try to persuade the bench officer regarding the meaning and significance of the evidence. It is the parties' opportunity to highlight key evidence and persuade the administrative bench officer to adopt a favorable interpretation.

Advocates should ask about closing arguments during the prehearing conference call or, if none is held, at the administrative hearing, before going on the record. The administrative bench officer might allow oral, written, or both types of closing argument.

Oral closing argument should be brief and persuasive. Posthearing briefs should summarize the facts and law in detail. In closing briefs, advocates may do the following:

- Cite to analogies and hypotheticals
- Comment on witness credibility
- Explain how the evidence fits into the party's overall theory of the case
- Argue why the administrative bench officer should decide the case in a favorable way

Trial Tip
Before going on the record, ask the administrative bench officer about closing argument—specifically, how much time he or she will allow. Sometimes, bench officers deduct time from oral closing argument if a party elects to put on a rebuttal case. It is best to clarify as early in the process as possible.

---

12. *State v. Childress*, 698 S.W.2d 612 (Mo. App. 1985).

13. A party in its case-in-chief is not required to call every possible witness who might possibly contradict every possible defense that could be raised by the other side (*Chrisler v. Holiday Valley, Inc.*, 580 S.W. 2d 309 (Mo. App. 1979)).

Administrative Hearing Traps to Avoid

Although administrative tribunals appear to be less-formal settings than standard civil court, do not be fooled. The stakes are high, the matters in litigation have consequences, expensive lawyers are spending client money, and administrative bench officers are drafting final determinations. Because the process is more flexible than traditional civil trial proceedings, parties and their counsel must be more vigilant, more proactive, more thoughtful, more strategic, and more well-prepared, not less.

Administrative bench officers have much more discretion than many advocates realize. Be helpful, respectful, and professional at all times. Address the administrative bench officer as "Your Honor," unless specifically directed otherwise. Advise clients similarly.

Remember to avoid ex parte communications. Try to use the administrative bench officer's staff regarding communications about scheduling a teleconference call with all counsel (or unrepresented parties) and the administrative bench officer to discuss issues. The administrative bench officer might direct parties to copy everyone on an e-mail to discuss the issues through group text. Check with the officer's staff before committing to a course of action.

Plan for travel, parking, and location signage failures; they will occur, guaranteed. Plan to arrive 45 minutes early. Build in extra time when scheduling co-counsel, clients, witnesses, court reporters, technology assistants, and everyone else.

Never try to be funny; try never to get angry. Neither advances the case.

Ethical Advocacy: A Heads-Up for Lawyers Advocating in Administrative Tribunals

Federal Agencies

All licensed attorneys who practice before federal agencies must comply with both the agencies' particular ethics rules for lawyers advocating in agency tribunals and counsel's individual state ethics rules for the state in which counsel is licensed.

Some specific agency ethics rules apply in disparate ways, at times, depending on which interest the agency is serving during counsel's advocacy in that forum. Generally, the broadest range of ethics rules applies when counsel is advocating before an agency as it engages in its adjudicative function.

Most of the specific agency ethics rules fill in around the state ethics rules and generally focus on the adjudicative process. Counsel should check with the agency to be sure to have updated ethics rules. This exercise would go a long way toward smoothing the path when counsel engages in zealous advocacy that publicly challenges the government's actions.

State Agencies

Counsel advocating before state agencies must comply with the ethics rules of the state in which the tribunal is held. As well, counsel should always be in compliance with counsel's ethics obligations in the state in which counsel maintains an active licensure.

Although, at first glance, counsel's compliance with all the ethics rules of counsel's states of licensure, as well as all the specific rules of each agency, may seem daunting if not impossible, the reality is that almost all ethics rules are based on the Model Rules promulgated by the American Bar Association.

8

After the Hearing

Leaving the Record Open

The administrative record can be left open for a specific purpose and a specific length of time. Only the administrative bench officer can decide to leave the record open. Counsel should be sure the request and the response are both on the record. Checking the statute to determine what (if any) posthearing submissions are officially permitted, and what procedures are required, is recommended.

Reasons to request that the administrative bench officer keep the record open include the following:

- To submit additional evidence
- To submit posthearing legal memoranda, particularly if problematic evidentiary or other issues arose at the hearing
- To submit posthearing briefs
- In extreme situations, to submit a sworn declaration or affidavit from an unavailable witness. Opposing counsel will subsequently need time to submit a written response to this submission

Trial Tip
After submitting posthearing material to the administrative bench officer, check with staff to confirm satisfactory receipt. Even if you received a return receipt with a signature through the U.S. mail, or received an automated notice through your computer's e-mail program that the message was opened, the material could still be misdirected or otherwise compromised. Better to be certain rather than blamed.

Posthearing Briefing

Counsel should read the procedures outlined in the agency's enabling statute or internal rules to see whether posthearing briefing is prohibited. Generally, posthearing briefing is permitted but must be kept to a fairly strict schedule so the administrative agency conforms to its own internal time restrictions for processing the file. To facilitate scheduling, counsel should be prepared with a calendar (with holidays, both public and religious).

Posthearing briefs are useful to address surprising or unfortunate evidence. Referencing documents in the record is a strong approach; counsel can cite to helpful witness testimony and explain away unhelpful evidence.

Trial Tip
Include case law and always check for new appellate decisions. Better-sourced arguments generally carry more weight in the eyes of the court.

Caveat
Never misquote, mischaracterize, or leave out important language from a reference. Administrative bench officers always catch on to this subterfuge.[1]   It never works in the citing party's favor.

Note
If an important new case that is relevant to your hearing comes down after briefs are submitted, contact the administrative bench officer's staff regarding supplemental briefing in light of the new decision or line of reasoning.   In some jurisdictions, counsel might be under an affirmative ethical obligation to do this. But if not, do it anyway.

An administrative advocate has done a good job representing the client when the bench officer's decision and order repeats language from counsel's posthearing brief. For this reason, counsel should write the document with the goal of helping the administrative bench officer craft a decision and order favoring the client's position.

---

1. An ethics violation in every jurisdiction in the United States.

Trial Tip

No clear consensus exists regarding footnotes versus endnotes or including references in the body of the text; ask the administrative bench officer to state a preference. As a general rule, the best practice is to keep the text flowing so the reading experience is the least fatiguing.

A popular compromise approach is to include the case name in the body of the text, placed at the end of the sentence, with the full citation in a footnote on the same page.

Example

"The burden of proof must be apportioned in strict conformity to the agency's enabling legislation . . ." (*Feds v. Smith*).[12]

Fn.12. *Feds v. Smith*, 101 F.3d 1247, 1251 (9th Cir. 1999).

Important points, central to your argument, should be included in the body of the text, not relegated to footnotes. Less-critical references, commentary, and asides should be in footnotes, which should be short and used sparingly, if at all.

Note

Endnotes tend to be disfavored in documents submitted to the court.

Exhaustion of Remedies

Generally, parties should exhaust all statutorily mandated administrative remedies before seeking judicial review in the courts. If exhaustion of remedies is required, requests for judicial review of administrative agency determinations in the absence of this process are premature and likely will be dismissed.

Exhaustion requires that moving parties pursue administrative processes to their ultimate conclusion; they must await a final outcome before seeking judicial review in civil court. Failure to appeal from an administrative decision to a higher administrative tribunal is generally a failure to exhaust administrative remedies.

Exceptions exist, however. Sometimes, litigants pursuing judicial review of agency actions under the federal Administrative Procedure Act (FAPA) need not exhaust available administrative remedies, unless exhaustion is specifically required by the enabling statute or an agency rule.

Failure to exhaust administrative remedies is generally an affirmative defense that can be waived. Waiver may occur if an agency does not raise the issue to the reviewing court.

In cases where exhaustion of administration remedies is not a statutory requirement, the court can apply its discretion. Courts can excuse the requirement in the following:

- Other remedies do not afford genuine opportunities for relief
- Irreparable injury may occur absent immediate judicial relief
- Administrative appeal would be futile
- The case raises a constitutional question that cannot be resolved through the administrative process.[2]

Exhaustion of administrative remedies may not be required if a party attacks an agency ordinance or rule as unconstitutional on its face.[3]

Note

If relief may be granted on nonconstitutional grounds, the court need not decide the constitutional issues, so exhaustion of remedies may be required. But if the administrative process does not adequately protect the constitutional rights at issue, exhaustion likely will not be required.

Caveat

Parties may not, by failing to submit issues of fact to administrative agencies, bypass this process. They cannot rely on the reviewing courts to decide issues that should have been considered by the agency.

Overview of Remedies

Remedies before an administrative agency tribunal are largely governed by the enabling statute for each agency. For this reason, the enabling statute is the first place counsel should check regarding permissible remedies.

Generally, absent specific limiting language, any appropriate relief, including declaratory relief, such as a declaratory judgment, is allowed.[4]

---

2. *Waste Connections, Inc. v. Okla. Dep't of Envtl. Quality*, 2002 OK 94 (2002).
3. *Sedlock v. Bd. of Trs.*, 367 Ill. App. 3d 526 (2006).
4. Model State Administrative Procedure Act (1981) § 5-117(b) (New Model Rules were propounded in 2010, significantly altering the approach to this topic; check the Model Rules adopted in your individual state, if any, before proceeding).

Declaratory Relief

A declaratory judgment is a determination of a court regarding the rights of parties.[5] The court does not order a party to do or pay anything in a declaratory judgment.

The validity or applicability of an administrative rule or regulation may be determined in an action for declaratory judgment if it is alleged that the rule interferes with or impairs, or threatens to interfere with or impair, the legal rights or privileges of the moving party.[6]

Declaratory relief is proper in cases where the moving party is challenging the authority of an administrative agency under the enabling statute and a determination on this point is in the public interest.

Note

Exhaustion of administrative remedies is generally not required[7] when the legal challenge focuses on the authority or power of an agency.

A declaratory judgment is a procedure to resolve controversies. It does not cancel the basic requirement that the moving party exhaust administrative remedies before seeking judicial relief in a civil court.[8]

In a case of actual controversy within its jurisdiction, in response to an appropriate pleading, any court of the United States may declare the rights (or other legal relations) of any interested party seeking such declaration, whether or not further relief is or could be sought.[9] Some exceptions apply, however, including tax actions.[10]

---

5. A declaratory judgment is a binding judgment from a court defining the legal relationship between parties and their rights in the matter before the court. A declaratory judgment does not provide for any enforcement, however. See *Roe v. Wade*, 410 U.S. 113 (1973); The Federal Rules of Civil Procedure (Rule 57) and Title 28 of the U.S. Code govern declaratory judgments in federal court.

6. Model State Administrative Procedure Act (1961) § 7 provides that "(t)he validity or applicability of a rule may be determined in an action for declaratory judgment . . ., if it is alleged that the rule, or its threatened application, interferes with or impairs, or threatens to interfere with or impair, the legal rights or privileges of the plaintiff. The agency shall be made a party to the action." (New Model Rules propounded in 1981 and 2010 significantly modified this topic; check Model Rules adopted by your individual state before proceeding).

7. *Construction Industries of Massachusetts v. Commissioner of Labor & Industries*, 406 Mass. 162 (1989).

8. Courts generally decline to reach the merits of a case when the moving party has not worked through the existing, available administrative procedures.

9. 28 U.S.C. § 2201 (2012).

10. Exceptions to obtaining declaratory relief include with respect to federal taxes (other than actions brought under § 7428 of the Internal Revenue Code of 1986 [26 U.S.C. § 7428]); proceedings under 11 U.S.C. § 505 or 11 U.S.C. § 1146; or in any civil action involving an antidumping or countervailing duty proceeding regarding a class or kind of merchandise of a free trade area country, as determined by the administering authority.

These declaratory findings have all the force and effect of a final judgment or decree. After notice and a hearing, further necessary or proper relief based on a declaratory judgment or decree may be granted. Relief may be had against any adverse party whose rights have been determined through this earlier declaratory judgment.[11]

Temporary Remedies and Stays

Unless prohibited by law, agencies may grant a request for a stay. The analysis is whether the terms requested are reasonable under the circumstances. Administrative agencies may grant other temporary remedies while judicial review is in process.[12]

During posthearing judicial review, a party may generally seek interlocutory review of an agency's action.[13] The moving party should apply for a stay, or other temporary remedy, generally by filing a motion in the reviewing court.

When faced with a motion for stay, reviewing courts are concerned with whether the agency's action cannot be supported or whether the circumstances are so significantly changed that the determination is no longer supportable. Assuming that an agency's action triggering a party's application for a stay (or other temporary remedy) is needed to protect against a serious threat to public health, safety, or welfare, the court may grant relief, but only if the following are true:

- The party seeking the stay is likely to win when the court rules on the underlying case.
- Without the stay, the party seeking the stay will suffer irreparable injury.
- Other parties in the case will not be substantially harmed if the court grants a stay.
- The agency's action is not justified by a threat to the public health, safety, or welfare.[14]

Once a court considers the appropriateness of a stay, it may issue an order or remand the matter to the agency, with directions to do one of the following:

- Deny the request for stay
- Grant a stay on appropriate terms
- Grant other temporary remedies

---

11. 28 U.S.C. § 2202 (2012).

12. Model State Administrative Procedure Act (1981) § 5-111 (The revised Model State Administrative Procedure Act of 2010 embodies § 5-111 in § 504).

13. An interlocutory appeal is an appeal of a trial court ruling, made before the trial concludes, asking an appellate court to review an aspect of the case.

14. The responsibility for decision making remains with the agency (*Bunce v. Secretary of State*, 239 Mich. App. 204 (1999)).

Injunctions

To secure an injunction, the barriers that a party must clear are high. For these reasons, reviewing courts rarely issue injunctions to stay administrative agency proceedings or decisions.

If a party's rights have been affected by the arbitrary or unreasonable action of an administrative agency, an injunction may be the proper remedy. If an agency has abused its discretionary power, the court may restrain it through injunctive relief.[15]

In contrast, reviewing courts must compel administrative agency action that the agency has unlawfully withheld or unreasonably delayed. A reviewing court must issue an injunction compelling an agency to take statutorily mandated action.[16]

Caveat
Reviewing courts have almost no equitable discretion to authorize noncompliance with statute; the exception is where a congressional moratorium on spending for that purpose bars the action at the time.[17]

Courts will not grant injunctive relief if the injunction will do the following:

- Contravene procedures mandated by Congress
- Interfere with ongoing agency functioning (the exception is where the agency has been found to have violated a party's constitutional or statutory rights, or a right created by a regulation)
- Affect what is determined to be solely a legal issue[18]

Money Damages

Money damages in lawsuits challenging administrative agency actions are generally not permitted, although a few exceptions have begun to crop up. The FAPA allows judicial review of objectionable agency determinations through actions for specific relief; these are not actions specifically for money damages.[19]

Parties who allege they have suffered financial damages from administrative agency action are entitled to judicial review of that action. If the issue is a claim solely for money damages, however, judicial review is not available.[20]

---

15. *Reed v. Civil Service Comm.*, 301 Mich. 137 (1942).
16. *Forest Guardians v. Babbitt*, 174 F.3d 1178 (10th Cir. 1999).
17. *Id.*, at 1178.
18. *Gibson v. Berryhill*, 411 U.S. 564 (1973); *Leedom v. Kyne*, 358 U.S. 184 (1958); *Myers v. Bethlehem Shipbuilding Corp.*, 303 U.S. 41 (1938).
19. Advocates should check the applicable state or territory APA to understand the contours of appellate practice in this regard.
20. 5 U.S.C. § 702 (2012).

However, money damages may still be recoverable: a federal court allowed damages for lost wages, loss of earning capacity, harm to reputation, and emotional distress (mental anguish). The court stated that although the petitioner was limited in seeking damages and presenting further evidence, the court would allow evidence and possibly recovery for these financially based claims.[21]

All Writs Act

The All Writs Act helps parties obtain interim relief in cases where administrative agencies abuse their power. Under the All Writs Act, federal courts are required to issue all writs that are essential or appropriate in aid of their jurisdiction and according to the usages and principles of law. A judge or a justice with jurisdiction shall issue an alternative writ.[22]

Note
The analysis is "evidence of abuse of discretion" (or some other inappropriate expression of judicial power).[23]

Arguments for Remedial Actions at the Hearing Stage

Bias or Prejudgment by Decision Makers

An administrative agency decision that is the result of biased decision making may violate due process as well as the FAPA (or state or territory APA). Agency adjudicators, including agency heads, have broad responsibilities, broader than just decision making. As a result, rules defining disqualification of administrative adjudicators for alleged bias are not identical to those for judges.

Bias or prejudgment exists if the decision-maker has:

- A personal interest (financial or otherwise) in the case
- Prejudged the facts of the case
- Before the hearing, developed animus toward one side, a particular witness, or counsel (or even a group to which they belong)

---

21. *Grosch v. Tunica County*, U.S. Dist. LEXIS 4966, 2009 WL 161856 (N.D. Miss. Jan. 22, 2009).
22. 28 U.S.C. § 1651 (2012).
23. *Cheney v. United States Dist. Court*, 542 U.S. 367 (2004).

> ## Caveat
>
> A claim of bias will not succeed just because the decision maker rejects the petitioner's claims, is not swayed by the testimony of a party, or holds unhelpful views on the applicable law, then-existing policies, or fact of the case not related to specific parties.[24]

Adjudicative decision makers must self-disqualify from deciding cases in which they are biased. But a petitioner's right to demand disqualification is waived if the party fails to submit a timely motion to disqualify.

> ## Note
>
> If a single member of a multimember administrative agency is biased yet participates in deciding a case, the agency's decision must be set aside. This is so even if the biased member's vote was not necessary to the final determination; the participation of the biased official affects the entire deliberative process.
>
> ### Example
> An administrative agency's adjudicative process requires two votes of a three-member panel. If all three members vote unanimously (3 to 0) on a file but one panel member subsequently is exposed as having been under a bias during the decision-making process, the entire agency determination must be overturned.
>
> Although, mathematically, the agency still has a majority vote on its decision (the two remaining panel members are still a majority of the three-member panel), the participation of the biased panel member affects the decisional calculus, and the resulting decision must be set aside.
>
> The biased panel member cannot simply drop out of the equation, leaving the agency decision intact.

Personal Responsibility of Decision Makers

Surprisingly, administrative agency decision makers are not required to personally attend hearings on files about which they are tasked to make a decision. Agency decision makers not present to hear evidence on a case may make a decision on the matter, but they must become personally familiar with the facts and arguments before participating.

---

24. *United Nurses Assn. of California v. National Labor Relations Board*, 31-CA-029713 (9th Cir. 2017) (NLRB No. 15-70920).

This can be accomplished by the following:

- Reading transcripts of the proceeding
- Reading briefs or memoranda submitted by the parties
- Hearing recorded oral argument
- Reading a report from a lower-level decision maker
- Reading staff summaries
- Being briefed by staff[25]

Caveat
Administrative agency decision makers enjoy a legal presumption that, when they make decisions on cases, they are personally familiar with the issues. Based on this presumption, absent affirmative evidence that the decision maker was unfamiliar with the issues, discovery regarding the extent to which agency decision makers familiarized themselves with the issues before making a decision is improper.

Improper Ex Parte Communications

Ex parte communication is any material, oral or written, relevant to the merits of an adjudicatory proceeding that was neither on the record nor on reasonable prior notice to all parties, that was exchanged between an interested person outside the agency (including counsel) and the administrative bench officer handling that proceeding, or a member of the agency, or a decision-making employee.[26]

Anyone not part of the administrative agency, who has an interest in the case,[27] may not make, or ask anyone else to make, an ex parte communication to an agency decision maker about the merits of a formal adjudication.[28] This restriction applies to decision-making members of the agency,[29] administrative bench officers, or any other employee who is, or might reasonably be expected to be, involved in decision making.

If an adjudicatory decision maker is subject to prohibited ex parte communication, a best practice within the administrative agency is to place the prohibited

---

25. Administrative agency decision makers may delegate decision making to lower-level officials only if permitted by law. Counsel should check the enabling statute for the agency for more specific information.
26. *Ex parte* communications, 12 C.F.R. § 263.9, *et seq.*
27. An interested person is someone with a stake in the case that is more specific than the concerns of members of the general public.
28. "Relevant to the merits of the proceeding" applies broadly. It encompasses more than just facts in issue (FAPA § 554(d)(1)). "Relevant to the merits" does not include requests for status updates.
29. The prohibition on ex parte contact applies to agency heads.

written communication in the record, or include a memorandum regarding an oral communication in the record, and include either written responses in the record or memoranda describing the substance of oral responses.

Note

The restriction on ex parte contact applies only to communications from entities outside the administrative agency.[30] Interagency staff communications to decision makers may be restricted by the separation of functions analysis but not by ex parte communication restrictions.[31]

Time Limits for Restrictions on Ex Parte Communication

Ex parte communications are prohibited starting at the earliest occurrence of any of the following:

- When the person responsible for the communication learns that an administrative agency hearing WILL BE noticed
- When the proceeding IS noticed for a hearing
- At the time the agency HAS designated for this purpose

If a prohibited communication occurs, all involved parties must disclose this fact.

Ex parte contact can be terminal to an administrative agency action. If an interested party engages in improper ex parte communication, the agency may demand that the party justify why the case (or the party's interest in the case) should not be extinguished. As another option, the agency may base adverse administrative findings on a party's knowing violation of the prohibition on ex parte communication. These processes must be in line with the policies of the enabling statute and the interests of justice.

If ex parte communication by an interested party reaches an administration agency decision maker, the agency's determination in the matter becomes voidable (a voidable act is an act that is valid but that may later be annulled or avoided by one of the parties to the act). But the agency's determination is not a void act (a void act is an act having no legal force or binding effect; a void act is a nullity).

Where ex parte communication has occurred and the administrative agency takes an action, the reviewing court examines whether problems with the agen-

---

30. The prohibition on ex parte communication is never a justification to withhold information from the government.
31. Although an agency is part of the executive branch, interestingly, the U.S. president is outside the agency for ex parte contact analyses.

cy's decision-making process render the agency's determination unfair to a party or hostile to the public interest.

Note
Limits on ex parte communications often do not directly apply to informal adjudications (those not involving administrative agency heads or bench officers). However, reviewing courts could overturn agency actions in which ex parte communication is present if the communication violated any applicable statute or seriously impaired a party's constitutional procedural due process rights.[32]

Legislative Interference with Agency Adjudication as an Ex Parte Communication

Any type of government pressure, subtle or otherwise, on administrative agency adjudicators to reach particular decisions may be prohibited as ex parte contact. In some situations, these contacts can violate fundamental rights.

Constitutional due process violation claims through ex parte communication are most effective if

- the contact seems to have influenced the decisional calculus of administrative agency adjudicators.
- the contact communication is about disputed facts (not law or policy).
- the contact served no legitimate adjudicatory purpose.

These types of interference with agency adjudication deprive participants of their constitutional right to due process or create a process that appears to the parties (and the public) to be a deprivation of constitutional due process rights. Both offend the Constitution.

Separation of Functions

If an administrative agency staff member participates on a file in an adversarial function (such as prosecution), this same staffer may not participate in (or even

---

32. "[A]n impartial decision maker" is an "essential" right in civil proceedings (*Goldberg v. Kelly*, 397 U.S. 254, 271 (1970)). "The neutrality requirement helps to guarantee that . . . property will not be taken on the basis of an erroneous or distorted conception of the facts or the law . . . At the same time, it preserves both the appearance and reality of fairness . . . by ensuring that no person will be deprived of his interests in the absence of a proceeding in which he may present his case with assurance that the arbiter is not predisposed to find against him." (*Marshall v. Jerrico*, 446 U.S. 238, 242 (1980); *Schweiker v. McClure*, 456 U.S. 188, 195 (1982)). Ex parte contacts foster neither impartiality and neutrality in decision making nor the appearance of such.

advise regarding) any adjudicatory decision in that case (or any other case that is factually related).[33]

Separation of functions requirements do not preclude administrative agency decision makers from participating in authorizing investigations, issuing complaints, or making other preliminary decisions, and later acting as the agency's decision maker in the same cases. Such requirements also do not prohibit agency heads (including members of multimember commissions) from personally engaging in adversarial acts, and later participating in adjudicatory decisions in the same (or a factually related) case. To qualify for this exemption, the individual must be an agency head both at the time of the investigation and at the time of the decision.

Note

Separation of functions restrictions do not apply to agencies deciding initial applications for licenses or to proceedings involving rates, facilities, or practices of public utilities or carriers.[34]

To ensure the soundness of constitutional due process, with few exceptions, administrative bench officers may not discuss the facts of any file off the record with agency staff, without notice to all parties, and an opportunity for all parties to be heard.[35]

To protect this independence and transparency, the functions of the administrative bench officer must be clearly and fully separated from an agency's investigatory apparatus. No agency investigator or prosecutor may advise an administrative bench officer on a fact issue, at either the agency review level or on appeal (except as a witness or counsel) in that proceeding or any factually related proceeding.

Note

Administrative bench officers may not be responsible to, subject to the supervision of, or work under the direction of an administrative agency staff member who is at the same time investigating or prosecuting matters for the agency.

---

33. Participation on a file means significant, direct personal participation in investigation, advocacy, or prosecution. Evelyn R. Sinaiko, *Due Process Rights of Participation in Administrative Rulemaking*, 63 Cal. L. Rev. 886 (1975), available at: http://scholarship.law.berkeley.edu/cgi/viewcontent.cgi?article=2493&context=californialawreview.
34. The American Bar Association, *Adjudication*, www.americanbar.org; http://www.americanbar.org/content/dam/aba/migrated/adminlaw/apa/blackletter1101.authcheckdam.doc (last visited September 25, 2017).
35. 27 C.F.R. § 71.98.

The Rule of Necessity

If disqualifying one or more decision makers results in the agency being unable to carry out its function, those decision makers should not be disqualified.[36]

Responding to the Decision and Order

Administrative agencies work on strict timelines, including getting decisions issued in a timely manner. Assuming the administrative bench officer leaves the hearing record open for a defined period of time (to receive posthearing briefs or other reason), the time in which the agency must issue its decision and order most likely will run from the date the record closes.

Counsel should doublecheck with the administrative bench officer regarding calculating the due date for the agency's decision and order, and calendar appropriately. This should be done on the record; if already off the record, the proceeding needs to get back on the record, so all parties can place the agreement on the record. This is important to avoid arguments from the other side that counsel has lost rights because of allegedly untimely submissions.

For various reasons, even if the administrative bench officer writes the decision and order immediately, because of administrative review and processing, it likely will come out very close to the due date.

Once the agency issues its decision and order, this triggers time limits in which counsel can request reconsideration or seek judicial review. Counsel should check the agency's rules about whether further administrative review is available, as well as the time periods for agency or judicial review. Calendar this date carefully. Timeframes can be surprisingly short (sometimes as short as 10 days), and some agencies and courts do not extend any leeway for materials filed late.

At this point, counsel might consider seeking advice from counsel who are more experienced with the post-administrative-hearing appellate process.

Counsel should analyze the impact of the decision. Is a party considering agency review or judicial review by a court? If so, consider submitting a timely notice to the agency or court regarding optional next steps, even if the client has not yet made a final decision about how to proceed. This preserves the client's rights and options while everyone absorbs the implications of the decision.

Counsel should research the appropriate standard of review. Different types of questions on appeal (factual, legal, procedural) are subject to differing standards of review. Sometimes, these various standards of review can coexist within a single appeal.

---

36. Pepperdine Digital Commons, *Is the Rule of Necessity Really Necessary in State Administrative Law: The Central Panel Solution*, www.digitalcommons.pepperdine.edu; http://digitalcommons.pepperdine.edu/naalj/vol19/iss2/3 (last visited September 25, 2017).

Trial Tip

Read the decision and order carefully to understand the compliance implications. If reconsideration or judicial review request paperwork is being filed, include a request for stay of enforcement, requesting in particular that no fees, fines, penalties, or interest accrue against the client during the pendency of the appeal or reconsideration process.

Include a research memorandum, declarations, and attachments to support the request for stay.[37]

---

37. For a sample of a complete federal request for stay pending appeal to an administrative agency, see Appendix C, Sample Stay by Food and Drug Administration.

9

Judicial Review

The information provided in this chapter is intended for educational guidance only on the complicated topic of judicial review, to help clients and counsel make smart joint decisions before reaching the judicial review level, regarding preserving their best arguments and positioning the underlying matter for the best chances on appeal.

Caveat
Judicial review is complicated and exacting. Counsel who are not appellate specialists should consult experienced appellate counsel for the appeal.

The Basics of Judicial Review

Appeals of administrative agency decisions to state or federal courts are known as requests for judicial review. Judicial review is the process by which courts examine the actions of agencies to consider whether these actions are consistent with the Constitution and the enabling statute and are not arbitrary. If the agency decision is reasonable, courts can approve the decision.[1] However, before approaching courts, parties generally must exhaust all administrative remedies.

On these grounds, reviewing courts could assume jurisdiction even when no specific statutory authorization for a judicial appeal is evident. Generally, in the

---

1. *McAlester Fuel Co. v. Carpenter*, 2009 Tex. App. LEXIS 1182 (Tex. App. Houston 1st Dist. Feb. 19, 2009).

absence of constitutional or statutory authority, a party has no inherent right to appeal from an administrative agency's decision and order.[2]

If an agency's enabling statute does not contemplate appeal from agency decisions, this does not violate due process rights. Even absent a statute providing for such relief or review, parties have a right of appeal from orders of administrative agencies if constitutional rights are involved.[3]

Federal Court Jurisdiction to Review Administrative Acts

The function of judicial review of administrative agency action is to opine regarding the following:

* The contours of agency authority
* Agency compliance with procedural requirements
* Whether the agency's action is arbitrary, capricious, or an abuse of discretion[4]

Reviewing courts look to see whether the administrative agency process was essentially fair. The court will determine whether the agency's action was not a rational application of statutory authority but rather solely an inappropriate expression of will.[5]

Generally, parties can resort to judicial review of an agency decision only after exhausting all administrative remedies.[6] This means that the matter should have gone through every stage of consideration and documentation before any party requests judicial review. A file usually cannot leap-frog over any stage of the process.

Claims or contentions not raised at the agency usually cannot be considered on judicial review. This rule provides for complete development of issues within the expertise of the agency. The agency's response to a party's challenge must be fully documented.[7] For the same reason, most theories or issues not raised at the agency level generally cannot be raised or considered on judicial review. Failure to raise an issue with the agency can preclude a party raising that issue for judicial review.[8]

Continuing the analysis, reviewing courts are usually precluded from considering objections not already raised with the agency. The agency must have an

---

2. *Springfield Fireworks, Inc. v. Ohio Dept. of Commerce, Div. of State Fire Marshal*, Franklin App. No. 03AP-330, 2003-Ohio-6940.
3. *American Beauty Homes Corp. v. Louisville & Jefferson County Planning & Zoning Com.*, 379 S.W. 2d 450 (Ky. App. 1964).
4. *Arrow Int'l v. Spire Biomedical*, 443 F. Supp. 2d 182 (D. Mass. 2006).
5. *Phillips v. Merit Systems Protection Bd.*, 666 F. Supp. 109, 110 (E.D. Tex. 1987).
6. *Island Bay Utilities, Inc. v. Alabama Dep't of Environmental Management*, 587 So. 2d 1210, 1212 (Ala. Civ. App. 1991).
7. *Hughes v. District of Columbia Dep't of Employment Services*, 498 A.2d 567, 570 (D.C. 1985).
8. *Personnel Bd. v. Heck*, 725 S.W. 2d 13, 17 (Ky. Ct. App. 1986).

opportunity to consider the entire matter, rule on the entire matter, and list the bases for its determination in the matter in its decision and order.[9]

For the same reasons, reviewing courts will not engage in fact-finding. All facts available to the reviewing court for consideration must be established and included in the record before the record closes at the administrative tribunal hearing level.[10] Only rarely will a reviewing court disturb the tribunal's determinations regarding witness credibility. Reviewing courts rarely intrude into the administrative bench officer's finding regarding what evidence predominates.[11]

Caveat

To preserve constitutional issues for possible later judicial review, counsel should raise the constitutional argument to the agency. This is true despite the fact that the agency does not make constitutional determinations.

Remember, if an issue is not raised with the agency, it might not later be considered for the first time as part of the judicial review process, with only a few exceptions.[12]

If a party fails to assert a constitutional issue at the agency level, the issue is waived.[13] But to preserve alleged agency error for judicial review, a party can raise a constitutional challenge for the first time in a petition for rehearing of an agency action.[14] That is considered raising the issue with the agency.[15]

In other words, whether a party has sufficiently raised an issue with an agency is determined by considering whether the party articulated the issued with sufficient specificity and clarity that the administrative tribunal was aware that it must decide the issue, and knew this within an adequate timeframe to make a decision.[16]

A party is considered to have raised an issue in an administrative proceeding to the extent necessary to preserve it for appeal in situations where a party provides more than just a hint or slight reference to the issue in the record.[17] The record must be sufficient to notify the court and the opposing party that the issue is in the mix.[18]

---

9. *Franklin v. Ark. Dep't of Human Servs.*, 319 Ark. 468, 472 (1995).
10. *Keyes v. N.C. DOT*, 684 S.E. 2d 65, 69 (N.C. Ct. App. 2009).
11. *Reisner v. Board of Trustees*, 203 N.W. 2d 812, 815 (Iowa 1973).
12. *Soo Line R.R. v. Iowa Dep't of Transp.*, 521 N.W. 2d 685, 688 (Iowa 1994).
13. *State v. Parks*, 290 N.C. 748, 751 (1976).
14. *Hughes v. District of Columbia Dep't of Employment Services*, 498 A.2d 567, 570 (D.C. 1985).
15. *Fisher v. Iowa Bd. of Optometry Examiners*, 478 N.W. 2d 609, 612 (Iowa 1991).
16. *Wallace v. Department of Air Force*, 879 F.2d 829, 832 (Fed. Cir. 1989).
17. *King County v. Wash. State Boundary Review Bd.*, 122 Wn. 2d 648, 670 (1993).
18. *Farley v. Town of Washburn*, 704 A.2d 347 (1997) (1997 ME 218).

Caveat

The general rule that an issue first must be raised before the administrative agency can be waived by the reviewing court by finding reasonable grounds for a party's failure to set forth the issue or assert the new grounds.[19]

Courts can consider newly raised issues if the court's failure to address them would deprive a party or the public of substantive constitutionally protected rights.

Reviewing courts have the power to determine issues that a party failed to raise to the administrative agency if the facts are undisputed and the issue is one that would result in an incorrect application of a statute. Three criteria guide reviewing courts considering whether an administrative agency's actions are reviewable:[20]

- The broad discretionary powers of the agency
- Whether the action implicates political, military, economic, or other choices not essentially legal in nature and, thus, whether the action is not readily susceptible to judicial review
- Whether the agency lacked jurisdiction, or the agency's decision resulted from improper influence, or the decision violates a constitutional, statutory, or regulatory requirement

The reviewing court decides questions of law and issues regarding validity of the law (questions of fact, policy, or discretion usually remain with the administrative agency).[21] Two types of administrative actions are judicially reviewable: actions that are expressly reviewable by statute, and actions for which no other adequate remedy in a court is accessible.[22]

Remedies Available Through Judicial Review

Remedies against the U.S. government itself are available.[23] Sovereign immunity is waived[24] when an appellant seeks nonmonetary relief,[25] but not all requests for monetary relief are considered requests for money damages in this context.[26]

---

19. *Pan American Petroleum Corp.*, 268 F.2d 827, 828 (10th Cir. 1959).
20. *Yeboah v. INS*, 2001 U.S. Dist. LEXIS 17360 (E.D. Pa. Oct. 26, 2001).
21. *Bowen v. Massachusetts*, 487 U.S. 879 (1988).
22. Administrative agency action made reviewable by statute and final agency action, for which no other adequate remedy exists in a court, are subject to judicial review. A preliminary, procedural, or intermediate agency action or ruling not directly reviewable is subject to review on the review of the final agency action. Except as otherwise expressly required by statute, agency action otherwise final is final for the purposes of this section whether or not there has been presented or determined an application for a declaratory order, for any form of reconsideration, or, unless the agency otherwise requires by rule and provides that the action meanwhile is inoperative, for an appeal to superior agency authority (5 U.S.C. § 704 (2012)).
23. *Kanemoto v. Reno*, 41 F.3d 641 (Fed. Cir. 1994).
24. A person suffering legal wrong because of agency action, or adversely affected or aggrieved by agency action within the meaning of a relevant statute, is entitled to judicial review (5 U.S.C. § 702, *et seq.* (2012); check for pocket part supplement before citing).
25. *Id.*
26. *Bowen v. Massachusetts*, 487 U.S. 879 (1988).

Courts must respect the integrity of the administrative process and should not look into the mental processes leading to agency decisions,[27] but substantial evidence must be present to support an administrative agency decision.[28] While deciding questions of law, interpreting constitutional and statutory provisions, and deciding the meaning of terms, the reviewing court may offer remedies such as compelling the agency to perform administrative actions that it is unlawfully withholding or unreasonably delaying, or setting aside an unlawful administrative action because it offends the law, is contrary to the Constitution, or exceeds statutory power.[29]

Reviewing courts can invalidate administrative agency decisions where government administration lapses into mere will, and can overrule regulations that are inconsistent with the language of the enabling statute or that are not reasonable implementations of the statute.

Generally, state APAs allow judicial review of an agency action by a court as the exclusive form of relief.[30] The action can be a rule making, contested case or other agency action.[31] If a state administrative review law applies, it may eliminate any other statutory, equitable, or common-law remedies that previously applied to administrative agency actions.[32]

Normally, a *mandamus* action in the appropriate court is available for ordinary "substantial evidence" judicial review of the adjudicatory administrative agency decisions, if no statutory provision for judicial review of final adjudicatory decisions by administrative agencies is present.[33]

Remedies Not Available by Statute

When an administrative agency's enabling statute does not confer a right of appeal, the remedy for improper official agency conduct is not judicial review. Parties should, instead, consider the following:

- Request for injunction
- Writ of *mandamus*[34]
- *Quo warranto* writ[35]

---

27. *U.S. v. Morgan*, 313 U.S. 409 (1941).
28. Substantial evidence is a degree of proof that reasonable minds consider adequate support for a conclusion. Nolo, *Legal Standards of Proof,* www.nolo.com; http://www.nolo.com/legal-encyclopedia/legal-standards-proof .html (last visited September 25, 2017).
29. *5 U.S.C. § 706 (2012);* check for pocket part supplement before citing.
30. *Heiland v. Dunnick,* 270 Kan. 663 (2001).
31. *IES Utilities, Inc. v. Iowa Dept. of Revenue and Finance,* 545 N.W. 2d 536 (Iowa 1996).
32. *Marsh v. Illinois Racing Bd.,* 179 Ill. 2d 488 (1997).
33. *State v. Maryland State Bd. of Contract Appeals,* 364 Md. 446 (2001).
34. A writ of mandamus is a judicial order to a court or a person requiring performance of a public or statutory duty (see *Cheney v. United States Dist. Court for D.C.,* 542 U.S. 367 (2004)).
35. A *quo warranto* writ requires a person to show authority for exercising the power relied on when taking an action; it does not evaluate quality of work or performance (see *First Nat. Bank in St. Louis v. Missouri,* 263 U.S. 640 (1924); Fed. R. Civ. P. 81(a)(4)).

Sovereign Immunity and Judicial Review

The United States, its states, and Native American tribes are all sovereign;[36] the sovereign is immune from lawsuits unless it has expressly waived such immunity and consented to be sued.[37] Waiver of sovereign immunity extends to all official misconduct by an administrative agency, not limited by the technical definition of agency action.[38]

When nonmonetary remedies are sought, sovereign immunity in suits for review of administrative agency action involving a federal question is waived under the FAPA.[39] The FAPA eliminates the sovereign immunity defense as a bar to judicial review of federal administrative action (assuming the action is otherwise subject to judicial review) and permits plaintiffs to name the United States, a federal administrative agency, or an agency head (or other appropriate official) as a defendant.[40]

Sovereign Immunity as a Bar to Judicial Review

Sovereign immunity bars the following:
- Assertion of federal question jurisdiction when a party seeks money damages
- Quiet title actions
- Challenges to the merits of underlying tax assessments

Judicial Review of State Agency Decisions

An agency's enabling statute must allow for an appeal,[41] and the appeal must conform to the statute; noncompliance results in dismissal. Statutory rules allowing appeal of agency decisions are strict and unwaivable; compliance with statutory provisions is essential.[42]

---

36. A sovereign is a government with supreme authority. In administrative appeals, the sovereign is the government body named as the defendant (state, federal, and tribal governments are considered sovereigns; counties are generally not considered sovereign).
37. Sovereign immunity is determined by the issues presented and the effect of the judgment, not by the party named as the defendant (*Bilger v. United States*, 2001 U.S. Dist. LEXIS 3236 (E.D. Cal. 2001); *New Mexico v. Regan*, 745 F.2d 1318 (10th Cir.1984)).
38. *Scheuneman v. United States*, 2007 U.S. Dist. LEXIS 93666 (C.D. Ill. 2007).
39. Where an individual seeks review of agency action, general waiver of sovereign immunity is set out in the federal Administrative Procedure Act 5 U.S.C. § 702 (2012). But this statutory waiver falls in the face of any other statute that grants consent to suit, which forbids (expressly or impliedly) the relief sought.
40. A U.S. territory is any region under the sovereign jurisdiction of the U.S. federal government. Puerto Rico, as a U.S. territory, is not considered a sovereign (*Puerto Rico v. Sanchez Valle*, 579 U.S. __ (2016)).
41. *In re Vandiford*, 56 N.C. App. 224 (1982).
42. For example, courts have no jurisdiction to hear appeals filed late. If the enabling statute limits the time for appeal from an administrative agency's decision, failure to file a timely appeal renders the late filing ineffective. *Cassella v. Department of Liquor Control*, 30 Conn. App. 738 (1993). If a statute accords exclusive jurisdiction to review an agency's decision to a particular, legislatively created panel, courts lack jurisdiction to review decisions of these agencies.

An enabling statute provides both an agency's source of power and the public's right of judicial review. The enabling statute defines the scope of a particular agency's power, which is considered by reviewing courts. Courts have no inherent appellate jurisdiction over official acts of a particular agency unless the enabling statute has provided for it.

The extent of an agency's power and a party's right of judicial review of an agency's decision are circumscribed by the following:

- The legislative history of the particular agency
- The objectives of the particular agency
- The structure of the statutory scheme
- The express language of the enabling statute
- The nature of the administrative action at issue

Subject-matter jurisdiction refers to the causes of action and the relief requested.[43] A jurisdiction challenge can be raised for the first time at any stage of the administrative process.[44]

Caveat

Parties must strictly respect the limits on the subject matter topics open to appeal that are set out in the administrative agency's enabling statute.

Jurisdiction and Venue

Statutes create (and limit) state courts' jurisdiction (power) to review administrative agency decisions.[45] Specified statutory procedures tend to show that the legislature intentionally crafted the procedures as the sole path for judicial review.[46] Appellant must file the petition for review in the statutorily designated venue.[47]

---

43. *State Tax Com. v. Administrative Hearing Comm.*, 641 S.W. 2d 69, 72 (Mo. 1982).
44. *State v. Rogers*, 172 S.W. 2d 940 (Mo. 1943).
45. Regarding judicial review of administrative action, district courts are courts of limited jurisdiction, with appellate jurisdiction to review administrative decisions only as provided by the legislature or constitution (see *Willows v. State*, 15 So. 3d 56 (La. 2009)). The district court's jurisdiction is limited to the time period set out in the applicable statute (*Molnar v. Mont. PSC*, 2008 MT 49 (Mont. 2008)).
46. If the statutory provisions are not sufficient, alternative provisions as to which court may be designated to review actions of administrative agencies are included in the Model State Administrative Procedure Act (1981) Article V, Judicial Review and Civil Enforcement.
47. Law.com, Definition of Venue, www.dictionary.law.com; http://dictionary.law.com/Default.aspx?selected=2216 (last visited September 25, 2017).

Otherwise, the court where the petition was filed does not have jurisdiction to hear the appeal.[48]

State courts scour the entire administrative record when reviewing agency decisions. State courts will overturn agency actions when

- the act violated statutory or constitutional provisions.
- the act exceeded the agency's statutory authority.
- the act was taken based on an unlawful procedure.
- the act was not supported by substantial evidence in the record.
- the act was arbitrary, capricious, or an abuse of discretion.[49]

Nonstatutory Bases of Jurisdiction for Judicial Review

There is no right to judicial review of an administrative order unless a statute provides that right or the administrative order adversely affects a vested property right or otherwise violates a constitutional right.[50] Administrative adjudications can be subject to judicial review through state legislative practice.

Two categories of judicial review of administrative actions are available: statutory and nonstatutory.

- *Statutory review*—Congress explicitly authorizes review of specified administrative actions. Statutory review generally precludes nonstatutory review, even if the statute is silent on this point.
- *Nonstatutory review*—consideration based on a statute that does not explicitly refer to an administrative action.

The exact contours of statutory preclusion of judicial review are gleaned from the structure of the overall statutory scheme, objectives, legislative history, and the nature of the administrative action involved, as well as the statutory language itself.[51]

Standing Related to Judicial Review

Standing to effectively secure judicial review of an administrative agency determination means that the party has an existing, substantial interest in the subject matter of the suit, which will be affected by the relief granted.[52]

---

48. Venue is either in the district that includes the state capital or where the petitioner resides or maintains a principal place of business, unless otherwise provided by law (if no law exists in the particular state jurisdiction, counsel should check the Model State Administrative Procedure Act (1981) § 5-104) (New Model Rules where propounded in 2010, significantly altering the approach to this topic; counsel should check the Model Rules or other rules adopted in the particular state before proceeding).
49. *Feasel v. Idaho Transp. Dep't (In re Driver's License Suspension of Feasel)*, 148 Idaho 312 (2009).
50. *Carlson v. City of Houston*, 309 S.W. 3d 579 (Tex. App.-Houston [14th Dist.] 2010).
51. *New York Univ. v. Autodesk, Inc.*, 466 F. Supp. 2d 563 (S.D.N.Y. 2006).
52. The analysis of whether a party has standing to secure judicial review in a federal court is found in Article III of the U.S. Constitution (see *Allen v. Wright*, 468 U.S. 737, 752 (1984)).

The U.S. Constitution restricts federal courts' judicial power to cases and controversies.[53] Under the FAPA, a person who is adversely affected or aggrieved by an agency action within the meaning of a relevant statute is entitled to judicial review. Individuals who merely have an interest in an issue are neither adversely affected nor aggrieved.

The party seeking review must allege injury in fact (actual or threatened) caused by the agency's action, which is

- to an interest arguably within the zone of interests to be protected, or
- regulated by the statutes or constitutional guarantees claimed to have been violated.

Prudential Standing

Plaintiffs seeking judicial review must also establish prudential standing by showing that the interest sought to be protected is within the zone of interests to be protected or regulated by the statute involved.[54]

The Model State Administrative Procedure Act (1981) provides standing to obtain judicial review of final (or nonfinal) agency action by the following:[55]

- One to whom the agency action is specifically directed
- One who was a party to the agency proceeding that led to the action
- One who was subject to a rule if the challenged agency action is a rule
- One who is eligible for standing under another provision of law
- One who would be otherwise aggrieved or adversely affected by the agency action

Types of Injury for Judicial Review

- *Injury-in-fact*. A person seeking judicial review must be adversely affected or aggrieved,[56] or have a direct stake in the outcome of a litigation (as distinct from those having a mere interest in the problem).[57] Injury may be economic or noneconomic.
- *Threatened injury-in-fact*. To have standing based on threatened injury-in-fact, a party must show that the agency's action likely will cause an injury

---

53. Cases and controversies limit federal courts to consideration of questions presented in an adversarial context and in a form historically viewed as subject to judicial resolution. Political questions, advisory opinions, issues that are moot, and parties lacking standing do not possess cases or controversies (*Alons v. Iowa Dist. Court*, 698 N.W. 2d 858 (Iowa 2005)).

54. § 10 of the FAPA requires that the party seeking review establish prudential standing; the interest sought to be protected must be within the "zone of interests" to be protected or regulated by the statute involved (*Dismas Charities, Inc. v. United States DOJ*, 401 F.3d 666 (6th Cir. 2005)).

55. § 5-106(a) of the Model State Administrative Procedure Act (1981) deals with standing of parties (the revised Model State Administrative Procedure Act of 2010 embodies § 5-106(a) in § 505).

56. *Warth v. Seldin*, 422 U.S. 490, 900 (1975).

57. *United States v. Students Challenging Regulatory Agency Procedures*, 412 U.S. 669, 690 (1973).

to a protected legal interest.[58] The alleged injury must be "sufficiently direct and palpable to allow a court to say with fair assurance that there is an actual controversy proper for judicial resolution."[59]

- *Economic injury-in-fact.* A competitive injury to business flowing from government regulation is an injury-in-fact sufficient to confer standing. But the mere possibility of financial loss because of lawful competition does not.
- *Noneconomic injury.* Standing "focuses on the party seeking to get his complaint before a federal court and not on the issues he wishes to have adjudicated."[60] Noneconomic injuries can support standing to challenge an administrative agency action.

Zone-of-Interests Test

The zone-of-interests analysis contemplates whether a party was properly heard, considering the legislature's intent when it made the agency's actions reviewable.[61]

Standing of Particular Entities

Parties may not assert the rights of others in federal court unless allowed by statute.[62] However, third-party standing is permitted when enforcement of an administrative restriction against a litigant prevents a third party (that has a constitutional right to contract with the litigant) from entering into a contractual relationship.[63]

Associations have a right to representational standing if they show that

- the organization's members would have standing to sue as individuals.
- the interests sought to be protected relate to the organization's purpose.
- neither the claim asserted nor the relief requested requires the participation of individual members in the lawsuit.[64]
- the injury meets the injury-in-fact requirement.
- the injury likely will be redressed by a favorable court decision.

---

58. *Romer v. Board of County Comm'rs*, 956 P.2d 566, 572 (Colo. 1998).
59. The personal injury may be "actual or threatened." (*O'Bryant v. Public Utils. Comm'n*, 778 P.2d 648, 653 (Colo. 1989); *Valley Forge Christian College v. Americans United for Separation of Church and State*, 454 U.S. 464 (1982)).
60. *Flast v. Cohen*, 392 U.S. 83 (1968).
61. The test "is not whether a party is in fact regulated by a statute, but whether that party asserts interests that arguably fall within the zone of interests so regulated." (*Apter v. Richardson*, 510 F.2d 351 (7th Cir. 1975); *Association of Data Processing Service Organizations v. Camp*, 397 U.S. 150, 153 (1970); *Clarke v. Securities Industry Assn.*, 479 U.S. 388, 399 (1987)).
62. *Valley Forge Christian College v. Americans United for Separation of Church and State, Inc.*, 454 U.S. 464 (1982).
63. *Secretary of State of Maryland v. Joseph H. Munson Co.*, 467 U.S. 947, 954-958 (1984).
64. *Hunt v. Washington State Apple Advertising Comm'n*, 432 U.S. 333 (1977).

Standing of States and Municipalities

States (and municipalities) with direct economic interests in matters have standing to challenge government officials' administrative actions. States have standing to challenge federal regulations that conflict with state law.[65]

Hobbs Act Standing for Judicial Review

A party opposing U.S. agency action can petition for review in a court of appeals.[66] Under the Hobbs Act, the federal appellate courts[67] have exclusive jurisdiction to enjoin, set aside, suspend (in whole or in part), or determine the validity of final orders, rules, or regulations (under certain circumstances) made by specific entities. Judicial review of an agency action is not available when the administrative agency has wide discretion in the matter.[68]

Note

Federal administrative agencies are aggrieved parties under the Hobbs Act, so they have standing to request judicial review of orders issued by other federal administrative agencies.

Note

Some federal administrative agencies' enabling statutes refer to the Hobbs Act for judicial review procedures.

The Scope of Judicial Review

Reviewing courts must set aside administrative agency actions if they are[69]

- arbitrary, capricious, an abuse of discretion, not in accord with law.
- contrary to constitutional right, power, privilege, or immunity.
- outside of statutory jurisdiction, authority, or limitations or short of statutory right.
- without observance of procedure required by law.

---

65. *State of Fla. v. Weinberger*, 492 F.2d 488 (5th Cir. 1974).
66. U.S. Cts., Federal Rules of Appellate Procedure (with forms), www.uscourts.gov; http://www.uscourts.gov/sites/default/files/Rules%20of%20Appellate%20Procedure (last visited September 25, 2017).
67. Except the U.S. Court of Appeals for the Federal Circuit.
68. The FAPA (28 U.S.C. § 2341 (2012); always check for updates before citing).
69. 5 U.S.C. § 706.

- unsupported by substantial evidence.
- unwarranted by the facts (to the extent that the facts are subject to trial *de novo* by the reviewing court),

Although a court can review administrative agency action with or without express authorization,[70] matters are not subject to judicial review if the agency is studying whether to take action on the file. For this reason, absent final agency action, agency orders are not reviewable (but courts must not interfere with legislative power, which would violate the separation of powers provision of the Constitution).[71]

Note

The judicial review provisions of the FAPA are not applicable if a statute excludes the review. States can statutorily exclude agencies from the administrative review process.

Type of Agency Action Affects Scope of Review
Fighting Judicial Review

Although judicial review of administrative actions is generally favored, judicial review of administrative agency actions can be avoided if it is clearly mentioned in a statute.[72] A legislature's desire to avoid judicial review in administrative actions should be clear from the language of the statute.[73] In most states, most administrative agency actions are presumed to be reviewable.

When preclusion of judicial review is implied from statutory language, courts interpret the extent of limits on judicial review.[74] Courts check legislative intent for guidance.[75] Absent legislative intent prohibiting judicial review in agency actions, a federal administrative agency cannot overrule the provisions of the FAPA.[76]

Courts can entertain matters for judicial review:

- If the administrative agency lacks jurisdiction
- If the agency makes decisions that are based on fraud or bribery or that violate constitutional, statutory, or regulatory commands
- If agency decisions are arbitrary and capricious, are an abuse of discretion, or are not in accordance with the law

---

70. *Save Hatton Canyon v. Skinner*, 1991 U.S. Dist. LEXIS 6627 (N.D. Cal. 1991).
71. *Western States Petroleum Assn. v. Superior Court*, 9 Cal. 4th 559 (1995).
72. *Block v. Community Nutrition Institute*, 467 U.S. 340 (1984).
73. *Gregoire v. Rumsfeld*, 463 F. Supp. 2d 1209 (W.D. Wash. 2006).
74. *Calabrese v. Chicago Park Dist.*, 294 Ill. App. 3d 1055 (1998).
75. *Dir., Dept of Labor and Indus. Rel. v. Kiewit Pacific Co.*, 104 Haw. 22 (Haw. Ct. App. 2004).
76. *Am. Soc'y of Cataract & Refractive Surgery v. Thompson*, 279 F.3d 447 (7th Cir. 2002).

> **Note**
>
> Decisions can be judicially reviewed, even if within an agency's statutory authority, if the agency does not provide reasons for a decision.

Administrative agency decisions that lack enforcement proceedings are not reviewable under the FAPA and are completely at the agency's discretion. These decisions are not reviewable; the legislature has evidenced no intent to limit the agency's discretionary power.

Courts can set aside disproportionate sanctions.[77] Administrative agencies may impose penalties; so long as they are reasonable, judicial review is largely precluded.[78]

Fighting Judicial Review: Nonreviewable Developments

Matters that are not "final agency actions" are not reviewable. Generally, judicial review can only follow an administrative agency's final order.[79] Agency action that is not final is generally not subject to judicial review.[80] An agency action is not final when the agency decides to assert original jurisdiction.[81]

Agency orders are not final when an agency

- eliminates the right to enforce a prior decision.
- determines liability but not damages.
- remands the case to the administrative bench officer for the taking of further evidence but awarding no compensation or monetary benefits.
- decides to propose legislation.
- drafts internal agency rules but should not confer on the petitioner the right to judicial review of cases that are not finally decided.
- Takes action that is tentative or merely the ruling of a subordinate official.[82]

Although an administrative agency's rule or regulation crafted under the FAPA is not an agency action proper for judicial review, when the rule is applied in a manner that harms a party, it becomes reviewable.[83] A statute can authorize creation of an administrative regulation, which can be reviewed.[84]

---

77. To determine the gravity of the penalty imposed, limited judicial review is allowed (*Matter of Pell v. Board of Education*, 34 N.Y. 2d 222 (1974); *Matter of Purdy v. Kreisberg*, 47 N.Y. 2d 354, 360 (1979)).
78. *Arthur Murray Studio, Inc. v. FTC*, 458 F.2d 622 (5th Cir. 1972).
79. *Digital Props. v. City of Plantation*, 121 F.3d 586 (11th Cir. 1997).
80. 5 U.S.C. § 704.
81. Original jurisdiction means the authority of an administrative tribunal to entertain a lawsuit, try it, and set forth a judgment on the law and facts (see *National Treasury Employees Union v. Federal Labor Relations Authority*, 712 F.2d 669 (D.C. Cir. 1983)).
82. The FAPA; *Dalton v. Specter*, 511 U.S. 462 (1994).
83. *Delano Farms Co. v. Cal. Table Grape Comm'n*, 2009 U.S. Dist. LEXIS 100093 (E.D. Cal. Oct. 27, 2009).
84. 5 U.S.C. § 702 (2012); check for pocket part supplement before citing.

When agency action is anticipated or when an action is pending for final consideration, judicial review can be denied. [85] Alleged problems in an agency's overall program cannot be judicially reviewed under the FAPA.[86] Agency decisions that expose parties to likely penalties are reviewable.[87] Under the FAPA, preliminary, procedural, or intermediate actions or rulings of an administrative agency, which generally cannot be reviewed in the interlocutory stage,[88] can be properly reviewed at the time of final agency action.[89]

Note

If an administrative agency action deprives a party of a constitutional right, interlocutory orders may be judicially reviewed.[90] Under the Model State Administrative Procedure Act (1981), which a number of states use as a model for their individual state APAs, a nonfinal agency action is reviewable only if the appellant likely will qualify for judicial review of the final agency action, and postponement of judicial review would cause irreparable harm.[91]

Ripeness of Question for Judicial Review

Administrative agency actions are not generally judicially reviewable until the action ripens into a mandatory obligation or denial of a right or freezes some legal relationship.[92] The ripeness doctrine protects administrative agencies from judicial interference before the agency can reach a final decision. Matters are not ripe for judicial review when the injuries are abstract, speculative, or have never occurred.[93]

To determine ripeness, courts consider whether

- delaying judicial review would cause hardship to a party.
- judicial intervention would interfere with further administrative action.

---

85. Agency actions that are not final are subject to interlocutory review only in extraordinary circumstances; a clear violation of law is required (see *Gulf Oil Corp. v. United States Dep't of Energy*, 663 F.2d 296 (D.C. Cir. 1981).
86. 5 U.S.C. § 702.
87. The Declaratory Judgment Act (28 U.S.C. § 2201, *et seq.*) can provide remedies against threatened or pending administrative action (see *Stewart v. Hannon*, 1980 U.S. Dist. LEXIS 13016 (N.D. Ill. May 19, 1980)).
88. The interlocutory stage describes something done between the commencement and the end of a lawsuit or action, which decides some point or matter but which is not a final decision on the matter in issue (Free Dictionary by Farlex, Definition of Interlocutory, www.legal-dictioary.thefreedictionary.com; http://legal-dictionary.thefreedictionary.com/interlocutory (last visited September 25, 2017).
89. 5 U.S.C. § 704 (2012); check for pocket part supplement before citing.
90. A stay is an interlocutory order (not a final judgment) because it does not resolve issues that would determine the matter. A denial of a motion to intervene or a motion for summary judgment is not ordinarily reviewable except on review of the final agency action (but if a statute permits it, courts can intervene) (*Railroad Trainmen v. Baltimore & Ohio R. Co.*, 331 U.S. 519 (1947)).
91. *Columbia Broadcasting System, Inc. v. United States*, 316 U.S. 407 (1942).
92. *City of Fall River v. FERC*, 507 F.3d 1 (1st Cir. 2007).
93. *Nat'l Park Hospitality Ass'n v. DOI*, 538 U.S. 803 (2003).

- the courts can benefit from further factual development of the issues presented for final adjudication of a case.[94]
- the regulations have a direct and immediate impact on the parties.[95]

An administrative agency's failure to act can be a final agency action for judicial review purposes. In this situation, a claim against an agency is ripe for review if the agency clearly rejects a proposed course of action or delays unreasonably in responding to a request for action until the requested action would be ineffective.

Primary Jurisdiction Doctrine

Primary jurisdiction applies to claims that could have been addressed in civil court but are more efficiently analyzed first in an administrative setting.[96] Under the primary jurisdiction doctrine, courts do not decide a controversy involving a question within the jurisdiction of an administrative tribunal until after that tribunal issues its decision.[97] Courts consider the facts and decide whether applying the primary jurisdiction doctrine advances its underlying purpose.[98]

Courts send matters for administrative rulings and stay further judicial proceedings.[99]

Note

The primary jurisdiction doctrine does not apply in appeals contemplating only questions of law.[100]

Judicial Review of the Merits

Because administrative agency decisions include a rebuttable presumption they are valid, the petitioner/plaintiff bears the burden of proving error on judicial review.[101] Reviewing courts are not bound by agency statutory construction but

---

94. Courts also consider whether the agency's actions are final, whether legal issues are presented, and whether all administrative remedies are exhausted (*Schultz v. Warren County*, 249 S.W. 3d 898 (Mo. Ct. App. 2008)).

95. *Office of Communication of United Church of Christ v. FCC*, 826 F.2d 101 (D.C. Cir. 1987).

96. *Coolman v. SBC Communs., Inc.*, 2005 Cal. App. Unpub. LEXIS 534 (Cal. App. 2d Dist. Jan. 20, 2005).

97. *F.P. Corp. v. Tamarkin Co.*, 1992 U.S. Dist. LEXIS 17929 (N.D. Ohio Mar. 20, 1992).

98. *American Auto. Mfrs. Ass'n v. Massachusetts Dep't of Envtl. Protection*, 163 F.3d 74 (1st Cir. 1998).

99. When a court refers an issue to the administrative agency, the court has the option to retain jurisdiction or, if the parties would not be unfairly disadvantaged, dismiss the case without prejudice (*Turedi v. Coca Cola Co.*, 460 F. Supp. 2d 507 (S.D.N.Y. 2006)).

100. *Pan Am. Petroleum Corp. v. Superior Court of Del.*, 366 U.S. 656 (1961).

101. Petitioner sought review of a decision of respondent District of Columbia Department of Employment Services, which denied his claim under the District of Columbia Victims of Violent Crime Compensation Act of 1981 (D.C. Code Ann. § 3-401 *et seq.* (1988)). The court held that the appellant failed to carry its burden of demonstrating that the agency's factual findings were not supported by substantial evidence in the record: he failed to forward to the court the essential parts of the record. But the court did not affirm the agency's decision;

do respect the agency's interpretation. Reviewing courts do not conduct de novo inquiry into matters on review; a court's focus is not on reaching its own conclusions regarding proper disposition of the underlying administrative matter.

The presumption of validity for agency action can be rebutted on review if the action

- is unsupported by substantial evidence.
- is so wildly incorrect as to be outside the realm of statutory authorization.
- is otherwise unreasonable, arbitrary, or capricious.[102]

The reviewing court decides whether the appeal involves findings of fact or conclusions of law, as well as questions of jurisdiction. For legal questions, the standard of review is the substitution of judgment test; for questions of fact, substantial evidence is the test.

Note

The moving party cannot secure review of the administrative agency's alleged procedural errors, just by asserting that an error violates due process, if the moving party failed to raise these alleged errors before the agency.[103]

Example

Reviewing courts consider administrative agency action in light of the evidence before the agency at the time that it acted. If the record before the agency at the time it made its decision does not support the agency's action or if the reviewing court is unable to evaluate the agency's action on the available record, the court will remand the matter to the agency for further development.

Note

Appellant's burden of proof to rebut an administrative agency's decision includes providing a record sufficient to establish that the agency's decision was incorrect.

---

the factual findings recited did not provide a foundation upon which the agency's conclusion of law could be supported. The agency's error resulted from misinterpretation of the meaning of the law; as a result, the court vacated the agency's decision (which denied the injured party's claim for compensation) and properly remanded the matter to the agency for further proceedings (*Cooper v. District of Columbia Dep't of Employment Services*, 588 A.2d 1172 (D.C. 1991)).

102. *Kaufman v. State Dep't of Social & Rehabilitation Services*, 248 Kan. 951 (1991).
103. *Vargas v. U.S. Dep't of Immigration & Naturalization*, 831 F.2d 906 (9th Cir. 1987).

Mootness

Significance and Causes

The question of mootness matters because

- it shows that the case does not encompass a justiciable controversy, or
- it shows that, after the agency issued its final determination, an event took place that addresses the controversy.[104]

Developments that might cause mootness include the following:

- Subsequent legislation
- Events not put in motion by a party
- Conduct of the parties
- The agency grants the remedy sought on appeal

Exception to Mootness Bar: Capable of Repetition Yet Evading Review

The exception to the mootness dismissal rule is legal controversies "capable of repetition yet evading review." If parties have no legally cognizable interest in the litigation, courts still might engage in review.

The "capable of repetition yet evading review" doctrine is limited to situations in which the challenged action is too brief to be fully litigated, and the same complaining party will likely be subjected to the same action again.

Courts consider

- the public importance of the question presented.
- the potential effect of the ruling on the judicial system.
- the possibility of a similar effect on the plaintiff in the future.

Note

The "capable of repetition yet evading review" principle does not necessarily trigger judicial review of seemingly moot matters.[105]

---

104. The analysis is whether the facts alleged, under all the circumstances, demonstrate a substantial controversy between parties with adverse legal interests of sufficient immediacy and reality to trigger the need for a declaratory judgment (*MedImmune, Inc. v. Genentech, Inc.*, 549 U.S. 118 (2007)).

105. *Board of Education v. Connecticut Bd. of Labor Relations*, 205 Conn. 116 (1987).

Supersedeas and Stay of Proceedings on Review

"Supersedeas" is a writ commanding a stay[106] on enforcement pending legal proceedings on appeal. A stay or supersedeas writ should be granted as a matter of right if the agency action suspends or revokes a license, but the reviewing court must determine that this would not result in danger to public health, safety, or welfare.[107] Stays may be modified, revoked, or extended.[108]

Note

Enforcement of an administrative agency action is not automatically stayed based solely on filing the notice of appeal or a petition for review.

Four factors are analyzed to determine whether a stay of an administrative agency's order is warranted:[109]

- The likelihood that the party seeking the stay will eventually prevail on the merits on appeal
- The likelihood that the moving party will be irreparably harmed without a stay
- The concern that others will be harmed by a stay
- The public's interest in granting the stay[110]

A petition requesting a stay should set forth the following:

- The reasons the court should grant the relief requested
- The facts relied on
- Sworn testimony regarding facts in dispute
- The record

Affirm, Reverse, Remand, Vacate, or Modify

On judicial review, courts may reverse, modify, or vacate the action or remand a final agency action to the agency for further proceedings. The appellate court

---

106. A "stay" suspends legal process for a limited time.
107. Model State Administrative Procedure Act (1981) § 5-111(c)(4); new Model Rules were propounded in 2010, significantly altering the approach to this topic; check the Model Rules adopted in your individual state before proceeding.
108. 28 U.S.C. §§ 2112, 2349.
109. *Michigan Coalition of Radioactive Material Users, Inc. v. Griepentrog*, 945 F.2d 150 (6th Cir. Mich. 1991).
110. Requests for stay will be denied pending review where the agency's action is suspended by the agency, the agency action is subject to the approval of the president, review of the agency action is not permitted by statute, review procedures in the court of appeal are fully adequate to protect parties' rights, or evidence is absent.

evaluates the decision of the agency, not the decision of the lower court that reviewed the agency's decision.

Note

Under the Hobbs Act, a court of appeal that is reviewing an agency order has the authority to, on the petition, evidence, and proceedings set forth in the record on review, issue a judgment that

- determine the validity of, or
- enjoins, or
- sets aside, or
- suspends, in whole or in part, an agency order.

The court will affirm an administrative agency's decision if the decision is correct for any reason appearing in the record, even if the grounds stated in the decision appear erroneous. The court may reverse, vacate, or modify an order or decision of an agency if substantial rights of the petitioner(s) have been prejudiced because the administrative findings, inferences, conclusions, decisions, or order

- were in violation of constitutional or statutory provisions.
- exceeded the statutory authority or jurisdiction of the agency.
- were achieved through unlawful procedures.
- were affected by other error of law.
- were clearly wrong in view of reliable, probative, and substantial evidence on the record.
- were arbitrary or capricious or characterized by an abuse of discretion or a clearly unwarranted exercise of discretion.[111]
- did not afford the appellant a fair hearing.
- involve a decision for which the court cannot find any support.

Agency Discretion as a Basis for Review

Abuse of discretion is sometimes a basis for a court to set aside an agency action that it finds arbitrary, capricious, or an abuse of discretion. This appears most frequently in the following situations:

- The agency relied on factors that may not be taken into account (or ignored factors that must be taken into account).
- The action is not reasonably related to statutory purposes or requirements.

---

111. *Catholic Diocese of Great Falls-Billings v. Schumacher*, 2007 Mont. Dist. LEXIS 111 (Mont. Dist. Ct. 2007).

- The supporting facts are not present under the correct standard of review.
- The agency action does not include sufficient explanation or is based on faulty reasoning.
- The agency inexcusably failed to reasonably consider important aspects of the problems presented by the action (for example, costs, circumstances, facts).
- The action is inconsistent with prior agency policies or precedents (without justification).
- The agency failed to consider or adopt an important alternative solution (without justification).
- The agency failed to consider arguments of the parties.
- The agency has imposed a disproportionate sanction.
- The action does not reflect reasoned decision making.

10

Review of Best Practices for Administrative Hearing Mastery

Quick-Review Checklist

Before the Hearing

Read the Notice of Hearing (Both Sides)
Read relevant statutes and administrative rules. Calendar deadlines for submitting exhibits. Calendar the date and time of the hearing—plan to arrive early. Note parking and other participation logistics, including technology.

Read the Statutes and Rules for the Particular Hearing
Every agency relies on and references statutes and rules applicable to both substantive and procedural issues.

Read Agency Opinions Relevant to the Subject Matter and Procedure
Issues are addressed repetitively in administrative agency proceedings.

Submit Exhibits to the Administrative Tribunal and Opposing Counsel Through the Prescribed Method of Transmission
Do this in advance of telephone and other types of hearings, under applicable agency rules.

Contact Witnesses to Confirm Attendance at the Hearing
Confirm payment of appropriate appearance fees. Request subpoenas as needed (some witnesses cannot get off work without subpoena paperwork, and sometimes even with it).

Doublecheck Telephone Numbers and Back-Up Telephone Numbers for Parties and Witnesses Appearing by Telephone

Submit the contact information for these individuals to the administrative bench officer if he or she will be connecting the witnesses to the hearing.

Prepare Declarations and Affidavits if Witnesses Cannot Testify Live

Hearsay is generally admissible in administrative agency hearings, so written statements instead of live testimony are usually acceptable. Notify the administrative bench officer's staff and the other side that testimony will be coming in through sworn statements.

Doublecheck Your Burden of Proof and the Opposing Party's Burden of Proof, if Any

The burden of proof varies depending on the agency, the subject matter, and the procedural posture of the file. The governing statutes and rules state the respective burdens of proof.

Consider Ways to Shorten Your Presentation

Stipulations of fact to be read into the record, joint exhibits, and stipulations as to authenticity or admissibility (or both) can shorten presentations without compromising zealous advocacy. You probably need to get your entire case on and off in fairly short order.

After the Hearing

Read the Decision

Note the result; reread the analysis leading to that result. Note the next step for further appeals (each agency, and some divisions of larger agencies, have their own appeal processes), and calendar accordingly. The immediate next step may be appeal to the agency director or may be appeal to another agency. Or the administrative bench officer's decision may be the final agency action, in which case the next step would be appeal to a civil court. Written decisions usually include this information; if not, call the agency immediately.

Administrative Advocates, Beware! Tips and Traps for the Unwary

Advocates should not do the following:

- Fail to carefully read all hearing notice information (front and back). Do not fail to follow instructions to the letter. If you need to vary from the instructions, seek written permission, and offer a sound basis for the request.
- Fail to exhaust administrative remedies: exhaustion of available administrative remedies is generally a condition precedent to filing an appeal or petition for review. Sometimes, actions taken by a subordinate officer of an

agency must be appealed to the agency head within 10 days as part of the exhaustion of remedies.[1]

- File late pleadings. Some civil litigators get distracted by the informal appearance of the administrative hearing process and get lax about deadlines. Pleadings (responses to citations, allegations, or petitions) must be received for filing at the office of the agency within the time limits. Response times can be as short as 10 days; do not assume you know the deadline—always check!

- Fail to preserve issues or fail to introduce evidence before the agency. When a party fails to raise an issue (sometimes, even a constitutional issue) in an agency proceeding, the issue is waived. New issues and additional evidence generally cannot be considered for the first time in a judicial appeal.[2] Remember, you must develop your factual record at the administrative hearing; you cannot continue this process at the appellate level.[3]

- Guess about jurisdiction issues. Whether a state administrative agency's action is subject to challenge through the state's original or appellate jurisdiction is not always clear-cut. The analysis starts with researching whether a statute or court rule specific to the matter under review answers the query. An incorrect decision could result in waiver of appellate rights.

- Waste time on excessive background/ramp-up testimony. Time is limited; other hearings are queued up in the hall or on the phone. Get to the critical point as quickly as you can. Consider a technique where you identify the witness, then ask the ultimate question on the ultimate issue as the next question, then backfill with all the lead-up questions. This takes some confidence, so consider practicing this question set before trying it in a hearing for the first time.

- Submit duplicate proposed exhibits or multiple copies. This drains administrative resources and benefits no one.

- Get thrown by questions from the administrative bench officer for client or counsel. Bench officers are obligated to develop the record; they are considered the most experienced resource in the room.[4] Avoid repeating the administrative bench officer's questions on your inquiry. The administrative bench officer likely will ask more questions if one side is unrepresented. It is not a comment on you or the witness—prepare your witnesses accordingly.

- Lob lots of minor, repetitive objections: No jury is present. The administrative hearsay rule probably applies (generally, hearsay evidence is admissible in administrative proceedings but may not be the sole basis for the ultimate decision). Limit objections to truly problematic situations and be brief: "Objection: hearsay," "Objection: foundation," "Objection: relevance."

1. *Citizens Concerned About Taxes v. Department of Education*, 739 A.2d 1129 (Pa. Cmmw. Ct. 1999).
2. *R.J.W. v. Department of Human Services*, 139 A.3d 270 (Pa. Cmmw. Ct. 2016).
3. *Umedman v. Unemployment Compensation Board of Review*, 52 A.3d 558 (Pa. Cmmw. Ct. 2012).
4. *Baker v. Emp't Appeal Bd.*, 551 N.W.2d 646 (Iowa Ct. App. 1996).

Hearsay is usually allowed in administrative hearings, so this objection goes more to the weight (rather than the admissibility) of a lot of the evidence.

- Lapse into leading questions on direct examination. Powerful witness testimony comes from open-ended questions. Percipient fact witnesses must have direct, first-hand knowledge in order to testify.
- Pose questions calling for speculation; these are a waste of time. They provide no facts on which a decision in your client's favor can be based.
- Alienate agency counsel. Government lawyers are experts at push-back in administrative settings. This is not a fight you want to start. Try to continue a constructive relationship with a professional communication style in the context of zealous representation. This benefits your client when an opening for an advantageous negotiated resolution arises at some point during the proceedings.
- Omit client, counsel, or witness scheduling conflicts or preferences in appearance scheduling documents.
- Forget to request an interpreter, as needed. Request the specific language (and dialect) in writing in the request for hearing. If the agency does not provide interpreter services (it usually does not), at least it is on notice that interpreters and language challenges will be a part of the proceeding.
- Forget to notify the court if you think you will need more than one hour for your presentation, and the reason why (multiple witnesses, extensive exhibits, interpreters, disabilities that need accommodating). This avoids a truncated hearing requiring everyone to return weeks later.
- Fail to organize documentary evidence and provide the documents to the other party or provide them to the agency for distribution. Moving parties generally mark documents using letters; responding parties generally use numbers; joint exhibits can be marked as "Joint Exh. [Roman numeral]."
- Indulge in lax, lengthy cross-examination. Keep it targeted and tailored.

11

Special Issues in Administrative Advocacy

Licensure Hearings: A Distinct Type of Proceeding

Overview: License-Related Administrative Hearings

Most license discipline matters are decided through an administrative hearing process, usually tracking the federal Administrative Procedure Act (FAPA) or a state APA. Licensure hearings include basic due process involving the following:

- Written notice
- A hearing (if demanded by the licensee or one denied a license)
- An administrative bench officer to hear the matter

Responsibility for the final decision is with the licensing agency, board, bureau, or department. The agency, board, bureau, or department can always reject or modify the decision of the administrative bench officer, no matter what the decision.

Preliminary Procedures

If a party holds a professional license, the licensure hearing process begins when the agency, board, bureau, or department serves the licensee with a notice, sometimes called an accusation. The accusation states the government's intent to discipline the licensee and the basis for the proposed discipline.

If a party is an applicant for a license who has been denied that license, the government serves the applicant with a statement of issues or similar document. The statement outlines the reason why the applicant should be denied the license.

The accusation or statement of issues opens the administrative case. Documents outlining the individual's rights in the hearing process usually arrive with the accusation and statement of issues.

Caveat

To preserve the right to a hearing, a party must quickly file a notice of defense (response to accusation, or similar document) in response to the accusation or statement of issues. Response times can be surprisingly short, might not account for time for mailing, or otherwise contain damaging surprises.

Failure to respond in a timely manner can eliminate the right to be heard. Calendar carefully!

The Licensure Administrative Hearing

A licensure-related administrative hearing is somewhat formal and mimics the structure of civil litigation. An administrative bench officer runs the proceedings, a court reporter or recording captures the proceedings, and cases are generally presented by advocates with extensive specialized experience in licensure proceedings.

No jury is present, and the rules of evidence are not strictly applied. Counsel make opening statements, call and cross-examine witnesses, enter evidence into the record, and make closing legal and factual arguments both orally and in pos-thearing briefs.

Administrative bench officers rarely rule on the spot; they usually take matters under advisement. Decisions are usually due no later than 30 days after the hearing ends or the record closes, whichever is later.

Licensing agencies usually have 100 days (this can vary: counsel should check the procedures and regulations promulgated by the agency) to adopt the proposed decision of the administrative bench officer, to reject the proposed decision and substitute its own decision (which sometimes happens if the agency believes the administrative bench officer has been too harsh or too lenient or made mistakes in the decision), or let the proposed decision automatically become the final decision after 100 days have elapsed.

Note

The agency's decision, if not promptly reconsidered, could quickly become final. It then becomes reviewable only on appeal.

Avoiding a Licensure Hearing: Early Resolution Options

Formal licensure disciplinary actions or license denial actions can lead to negotiated resolutions. If so, the hearing is cancelled.

The negotiated resolution can be in the format of a stipulated settlement or something similar. Whatever the title of the document, the licensing agency agrees to drop a more severe punishment or back off denial of a license. The government agrees to this to secure early resolution of a case, with no risk exposure. The licensee or license applicant waives the right to a hearing to avoid the possibility of severe discipline or a final denial of a license after hearing.

Stipulated settlement terms vary widely depending on the agency, board, bureau, or department. Some cases are settled for a reprimand, but many are settled for probation. Probation often includes some type of stayed (suspended) penalty and specific tasks, such as educational classes, community service, or successful completion of treatment programs.

Trial Tip

You can ask, during negotiation of a resolution to avoid a hearing, that whatever the length of the licensee-client's probationary period may be, the time is calculated to have begun on the date of the notice, rather than the date of the negotiated resolution. This results in your client functionally being under the licensing board's supervision for a month or so less, putting the client back into a standard licensed posture a month or so earlier, which can enhance employability.

Note

During the probationary period under a negotiated resolution, violation of the terms of the settlement agreement usually trigger expedited summary imposition of the suspended or stayed punishment.

Fifth Amendment Rights at Administrative Hearings

A licensee or person denied a license has no right to remain silent at a licensure hearing unless the party invokes the Fifth Amendment constitutional right against self-incrimination. However, if the licensee or license applicant does not voluntarily take the stand and testify, the licensing agency advocate can call the witness to the stand, where the witness must expressly invoke Fifth Amendment protections.

After the Licensure Hearing

Before the decision becomes final, a licensee or license applicant can request an agency to reconsider its decision. The focus of the reconsideration process is to

- point out defects in the administrative decision.
- raise new evidence and legal arguments.
- raise objections before the administrative matter closes.

Agencies sometimes delay a final decision's effective date to accommodate review under a petition for reconsideration. If the agency agrees to reconsider the decision, additional written or oral arguments may be requested and considered before issuing a new decision. The agency can affirm or modify its prior decision.

Once the reconsideration phase is completed, appeals of administrative decisions are usually filed in Superior Court or the trial level of the local court system, requesting a writ of administrative mandamus. This appeal process is complicated and detail-heavy.[1] If the appellate decision overturns the agency decision, the matter is generally sent back to the agency with instructions.

Reinstating a License

Most agencies have promulgated rules governing license reinstatement.[2] Revoked licenses can be restored after a few years, in most cases, with a demonstration of insight regarding the underlying problematic conduct and a showing of rehabilitation. In this situation, licensees may not have to requalify for the license; rather, they appear and present at either an administrative hearing or at a licensing board meeting.

Note

Some agencies require that a disciplined former licensee reapply for the license to start the reinstatement process, including paying application and testing fees.

Telephone Hearings

The volume of administrative hearings has steadily increased since the 1960s; agencies more and more often rely on technology to meet their workloads. This has included telephone and other tele-hearings for many years.

---

1. Parties must prepare the administrative hearing record and submit timely legal briefs. Appellate hearings often require oral argument.
2. For example, under the Nevada State Bar rules, disbarred attorneys may not petition for reinstatement for a minimum of three years from the effective date of disbarment. Reinstatement, if granted by the court, requires proof of fitness to practice law and satisfaction of any conditions imposed by the court (for example, passing the bar exam and/or the ethics exam, paying restitution, completing probation, or other requirement).

It is generally accepted that tele-hearings provide parties with a full and fair hearing, with adequate opportunity to present evidence, confront and cross-examine witnesses, and judge the credibility of witnesses.[3] For this reason, the chances are high that administrative litigators will confront this process at some point.

Telephone hearings have long been used in unemployment compensation, drivers' licensing, and human services hearings. Best practices assure that the telephone hearing is fair, the process is efficient, and the decision produced by the telephone hearing is accurate.

Before the Telephone Hearing

Telephone hearing notices inform the parties of how the process will be initiated. Sometimes, parties are provided a telephone conference number to call, with access allowed when they enter the numeric code provided on the notice of telephonic hearing. In other systems, parties must provide counsel's, client's, and witnesses' telephone numbers to the agency in advance of the hearing.

Some advanced automated telephone hearing systems allow parties to provide (and change) their phone numbers online. This web-based system then autodials the participants for the hearing.

The hearing notice includes instructions for submitting exhibits before the hearing. This is an important deadline to calendar because the agency needs time to log the evidentiary submissions and send them to the other side before the hearing. Documents and pages should be numbered so that they can be referenced and easily located by all telephonic hearing participants. This helps ensure a clear and understandable record of the proceedings for posthearing briefing or appeal.

During the Telephone Hearing

Administrative bench officers begin tele-hearings with an explanation of the telephone hearing process. The administrative bench officer should provide participants with instructions for rejoining the tele-hearing and what participants should do if they become disconnected.

Everyone offering evidence in a tele-hearing is testifying under oath; they cannot be prompted by other hearing participants. The administrative bench officer will request that all participants speaking during the hearing identify themselves for the recording.

Participants are not allowed to interrupt any other participant, with the exception of legal objections. Clients and witnesses should be prepared for participation, including an understanding of these unique hearings.

---

3. *Mathews v Eldridge*, 424 U.S. 319 (1976).

After the Telephone Hearing

Decisions are e-mailed or sent by post to counsel within a statutory timeframe. Most likely, written requests to preserve the recording of the hearing must be made almost immediately. The request probably costs nothing and preserves the record for reconsideration and appeal, if desired.

Caveat

Administrative agencies with high-volume hearing calendars do not have the capacity to preserve hearing tapes, no matter how compressed the format.

Do not assume that anything will happen automatically. Get your written request for the record, reconsideration, or anything else to the proper agency employee right away.

Appendix A: Forms

Administrative Hearing Cross-Examination Form

Confidential/Attorney Work Product/Do Not Forward/ Do Not Circulate Index of Exhibits

Case Name

Feds v. Smith

Exh. #	Description	Witness	Offered (Date/Time)	Accepted	Rejected	Notes

Evidence Tracking Form

Confidential/Attorney Work Product/Do Not Forward/ Do Not Circulate Index of Exhibits

Case Name

Feds v. Smith

Focus: recollection immediately after event (2/8 statement) v. different recollection after consult with counsel (7/15 discover)

Docs: E-mails (Ex. 3, Ex. 5, Ex. 7), Tr. Of I/V (Ex. 12), signed affidavit (Ex. 32)

DIRECT TESTIMONY	QUESTIONS FOR CROSS-EXAM or FOLLOW-UP
Q: _____	Q: _____
A: _____	A: _____
Q: _____	Q: _____
A: _____	A: _____
Q: _____	Q: _____
A: _____	A: _____
Q: _____	Q: _____
A: _____	A: _____
Q: _____	Q: _____
A: _____	A: _____
Q: _____	Q: _____
A: _____	A: _____

Appendix B: For Further Reference

Administrative Law Sources and Reference Guides

Guide to Administrative Law, Law Library of Congress: https://www.loc.gov/law/help/administrative.php

Harvard Law School Library, Administrative Law Research, Administrative and Regulatory Law Research Guide: guides.library.harvard.edu/administrative

Administrative Agencies

A-Z Index of U.S. Government Departments and Agencies: https://www.usa.gov/federal-agencies/

List of all California agencies: http://www.ca.gov/Agencies

List of Texas state agencies: Texas Records and Information Locator (TRAIL) List of Texas State Agencies: https://www.tsl.texas.gov/apps/lrs/agencies/index.html

List of all Florida administrative agencies: https://dos.myflorida.com/library-archives/research/florida-information/government/state-resources/state-agency-homepages/

List of New York administrative agencies: https://www.ny.gov/agencies

List of Illinois administrative agencies: https://www2.illinois.gov/agencies

Federal and State Constitutions

The Constitution of the United States: A Transcription, National Archives: https://www.archives.gov/founding-docs/constitution-transcript

California State Constitution: http://www.leginfo.ca.gov/const-toc.html

Texas State Constitution: http://www.constitution.legis.state.tx.us/

Florida State Constitution: http://www.leg.state.fl.us/statutes/index.cfm?submenu=3

New York Constitution: https://www.dos.ny.gov/info/constitution.htm

Illinois Constitution: http://www.ilga.gov/commission/lrb/conent.htm

State and Federal Acts Addressing Administrative Law and Procedure

Federal Administrative Procedure Act (5 U.S.C. Subchapter II), National Archives: https://www.archives.gov/federal-register/laws/administrative-procedure

California Administrative Procedure Act: https://oal.ca.gov/publications/administrative_procedure_act/

Texas Administrative Procedure Act: http://www.statutes.legis.state.tx.us/Docs/GV/htm/GV.2001.htm

Florida Administrative Procedure Act: http://www.leg.state.fl.us/Statutes/index.cfm?App_mode=Display_Statute&URL=0100-0199/0120/0120.html

New York Administrative Procedure Act: https://www.nysenate.gov/legislation/laws/SAP

Illinois Administrative Procedure Act: http://www.ilga.gov/legislation/ilcs/ilcs5.asp?ActID=83&ChapterID=2

Unfunded Mandates Reform Act, found online at: https://www.gsa.gov/policy-regulations/policy/federal-advisory-committee-management/legislation-and-regulations/unfunded-mandates-reform-act

Negotiated Rulemaking and Alternative Dispute Resolution Acts, The Negotiated Rulemaking Act of 1996, Pub. Law 104-320 (amending Pub. Law 101-648 and Pub. Law 102-354), Title 5 U.S.C. Subchapter III – Negotiated Rulemaking Procedure: https://www.epa.gov/sites/production/files/2015-09/documents/regnegact.pdf

Congressional Review Act: https://www.senate.gov/CRSpubs/316e2dc1-fc69-43cc-979a-dfc24d784c08.pdf

Data Quality Act (DQA) or Information Quality Act (IQA), U.S. Department of State: https://www.state.gov/misc/49492.htm

The E-Government Act of 2002, U.S. Department of Justice: https://www.justice.gov/opcl/e-government-act-2002

Appendix C: Sample Stay by Food and Drug Administration[1]

---

1. Note: This stay is provided as an illustrative example, not a guide. Readers should be sure of and comply with the rules applicable in their own cases.

Case 1:12-cv-00763-ERK-VVP   Document 91-1   Filed 05/01/13   Page 1 of 17 PageID #: 2201

UNITED STATES DISTRICT COURT
EASTERN DISTRICT OF NEW YORK

Annie TUMMINO, *et al.*,)	
)	
Plaintiffs,)	No. 12-CV-763 (ERK/VVP)
v.)	
)	(Korman, J.)
Dr. Margaret HAMBURG, Commissioner of)	(Pohorelsky, M.J.)
Food and Drugs, *et al.*,)	
)	
Defendants.)	

MEMORANDUM IN SUPPORT OF DEFENDANTS' MOTION FOR STAY PENDING APPEAL

By its Order dated April 5, 2013 (ECF #85), and judgment entered on April 10, 2013 (ECF #87), this Court entered a mandatory injunction directing the Food and Drug Administration (FDA): "to grant the Citizen Petition and make levonorgestrel-based emergency contraceptives available without a prescription and without point-of-sale or age restrictions within thirty days. On remand, the FDA may determine whether any new labeling is reasonably necessary. Moreover, if the FDA actually believes there is any significant difference between the one- and two-pill products [Plan B One-Step and Plan B, respectively], it may limit its over-the-counter approval to the one-pill product." *Tummino v. Hamburg*, __ F. Supp. 2d __, No. 12-763, 2013 WL 1348656, at *31 (E.D.N.Y. Apr. 5, 2013) (hereinafter *Tummino II*). Defendants have filed a notice of appeal to the Second Circuit from the Order and judgment. Pursuant to Fed. R. Civ. P. 62(c) and Fed. R. App. P. 8(a)(1)(A), (C), defendants respectfully move the Court to stay its Order and judgment pending appeal.

If the Court is not inclined to grant our motion for a stay pending appeal, the government moves for a temporary administrative stay of the Court's Order and judgment pending resolution by the Court of Appeals of a stay motion to that court under FRAP 8(a)(2).

Such an administrative stay would allow both this Court and the Court of Appeals to consider a stay pending appeal on a non-emergency basis, with full briefing. If this Court enters a temporary administrative stay but denies a stay pending appeal, defendants will promptly inform this Court of any Court of Appeals decision regarding a stay pending appeal. In view of the short time before the government is required to take steps to comply with the Court's order, which is effective on May 6, we respectfully request a ruling on the stay motion by the end of the day on Thursday, May 2, so that, if necessary, we may seek an emergency stay from the Court of Appeals.

The remedy the Court ordered was erroneous, for at least two reasons. First, the Court exceeded its authority by issuing an order concerning the "one-pill product," *i.e.*, Plan B One-Step (PBOS), a drug product that was not the subject of the Citizen Petition that is the basis of this action before the Court. Rather, PBOS was the subject of a supplemental new drug application (SNDA), and the Court recognized it "do[es] not have any authority to review the denial of the Plan B One-Step SNDA for the purpose of granting relief." *Tummino II*, 2013 WL 1348656, at *34. Second, the Court exceeded its authority, under principles of administrative law and the Federal Food, Drug, and Cosmetic Act (FDCA), by issuing a mandatory injunction ordering FDA "to make levonorgestrel-based emergency contraceptives available without a prescription and without point-of-sale or age restrictions within thirty days," rather than remanding to the agency for further administrative action. In such a situation, the appropriate remedy is to vacate an administrative agency's decision and to order the agency to reconsider its decision or provide a more complete explanation. The Court cannot pretermit the rulemaking process and foreclose public participation in that process by instead immediately mandating a particular substantive outcome. As set forth below, in view of these errors, the government has a substantial likelihood of success on appeal, and the balance of harms tips decidedly in the government's favor. Accordingly, it is entitled to a stay pending appeal.

A stay will not harm the plaintiffs because all of them are at least 15 years old and will soon be able to obtain at least one emergency contraceptive containing levonorgestrel (*viz.*, PBOS) without a prescription, and without having to request that drug from behind the pharmacy counter, at retail establishments that have a pharmacy counter, whether or not the pharmacy counter is open. On April 30, 2013, FDA approved an amended SNDA that had been submitted earlier by Teva Branded Pharmaceutical Products R&D, Inc. (Teva), to seek to market PBOS with no prescription requirements for any consumer but with a labeling restriction providing that the drug is not intended for use by, or sale to, consumers under age 15. *See* Decl. of Dr. Janet Woodcock, Director, FDA Center for Drug Evaluation and Research ¶ 3 (annexed hereto as Exhibit A). In that amended SNDA that FDA has now approved, Teva indicated that it will distribute PBOS to retailers with an on-site pharmacy, where it may be placed in the family planning or female health aisle (rather than kept behind the pharmacy counter) and may be sold during the retailer's normal operating hours, whether or not the pharmacy is open. The approved packaging will state that the drug is "not for sale to those under 15 years of age | proof of age required | not for sale where age cannot be verified," and the UPC code will prompt the cashier to request proof of age. The current approval does not include the lawful marketing of a prescription product for younger age groups, so the previous "dual marketing regime" for that product would end. *Id.*[1]

Teva had submitted that amended SNDA before the Court issued its April 5 Order,[2] and FDA's approval of the amended SNDA was not undertaken to comply with that Order.[3] *Id.* Thus,

---

[1] For persons under 15 years old, generic equivalents of Plan B, containing the two-pill levonorgestrel-based emergency contraceptive, remain available with a prescription. Woodcock Decl. ¶ 3(f).

[2] FDA does not generally disclose the existence of an application before approval absent permission from or disclosure by the sponsor. 21 C.F.R. § 314.430.

[3] As the Court is aware, FDA issued a complete response letter to the PBOS sponsor on December 7, 2011, in response to its February 7, 2011, SNDA (agency docket no. 21-998/S-002), which sought to classify

the approval does not and was not intended to provide all of the relief that the Court required in the Order, but instead reflects FDA's judgment that Teva's application contained appropriate scientific data demonstrating that the product was safe and effective for nonprescription use for females ages 15 and up. Upon approving the amended SNDA, FDA granted Teva three years of marketing exclusivity for PBOS on the basis of actual use studies that Teva conducted in women age 15 and 16 that FDA found essential to approval. *Id.* FDA's approval of the amended SNDA affects only PBOS, and does not affect Plan B or its generic equivalents, which remain available without a prescription to women age 17 and older, and by prescription to women under 17.

STANDARD FOR A STAY PENDING APPEAL

Rule 62(c) of the Federal Rules of Civil Procedure provides that "[w]hile an appeal is pending from an interlocutory order or final judgment that grants, dissolves, or denies an injunction, the court may suspend, modify, restore, or grant an injunction." In this Circuit, four factors are considered before granting a stay pending appeal: "(1) whether the movant will suffer irreparable injury absent a stay, (2) whether a party will suffer irreparable injury if a stay is issued, (3) whether the movant has demonstrated a substantial possibility, although less than a likelihood, of success on appeal, and (4) the public interests that may be affected." *Torres v. New York State Bd. of Elections*, 462 F.3d 161, 207 (2d Cir. 2006) (quoting *Hirschfeld v. Board of Elections*, 984 F.2d 35, 39 (2d Cir. 1993)); *see also In re World Trade Center Disaster Site Litig.*, 503 F.3d 167, 170-71 (2d Cir. 2007). In *Mohammed v. Reno*, 309 F.3d 95 (2d Cir. 2002), the Second Circuit surveyed how different courts have analyzed the prospect of success necessary for issuing

---

PBOS as an over-the-counter (OTC) drug product for consumers of all ages. However, the issuance of the complete response letter was not the definitive end of FDA's administrative process with respect to the prescription status of PBOS. As defendants have explained, after receiving a complete response letter, a drug sponsor has several options: it may withdraw its application, 21 C.F.R. § 14.110(b)(2); it may request an agency hearing, *id.* § 314.110(b)(3); it may seek review in the Court of Appeals, 21 U.S.C. § 355(h); or it may revise its application — for example, by amending the request — and resubmit it for approval, 21 C.F.R. § 314.110(b)(1). Here, Teva responded to the complete response letter by amending and resubmitting its SNDA to FDA. *See* Woodcock Decl. ¶ 3.

a stay, ultimately agreeing with the District of Columbia Circuit's approach, whereby "[t]he necessary 'level' or 'degree' of possibility of success will vary according to the Court's assessment of the other [stay] factors." *Id.* at 101 (quoting *Washington Metro. Area Transit Comm'n v. Holiday Tours, Inc.*, 559 F.2d 841, 843 (D.C. Cir. 1977)). The Court observed: "[t]he probability of success that must be demonstrated is inversely proportional to the amount of irreparable injury plaintiff will suffer absent the stay. Simply stated, more of one excuses less of the other." *Mohammed*, 309 F.3d at 101 (citing *Washington Metro. Area Transit Comm'n*, 559 F.2d at 843); *see also Citigroup Global Markets, Inc. v. VCG Special Opportunities Master Fund, Ltd.*, 598 F.3d 30, 36-38 & n.8 (2d Cir. 2010); *NRDC v. FDA*, 884 F. Supp. 2d 108, 121-23 (S.D.N.Y. 2012); *Safeco Ins. Co. of America v. M.E.S., Inc.*, No. 09-CV-3312 (ARR), 2010 WL 5437208, at *7 (E.D.N.Y. Dec. 17, 2010) (collecting cases indicating that the party seeking a stay does not need to demonstrate that it is more likely than not that it will succeed on the merits).

ARGUMENT

I.   **DEFENDANTS HAVE A SUBSTANTIAL LIKELIHOOD OF SUCCESS ON APPEAL.**

    A.   **The Court Exceeded its Subject Matter Jurisdiction in Reviewing the Agency's Denial of Teva's SNDA for PBOS and Ordering Agency Approval of PBOS for Unrestricted OTC Availability.**

This Court lacks subject matter jurisdiction to review any aspect of Teva's February 2011 SNDA for PBOS, including the HHS Secretary's December 2011 directive to the FDA Commissioner to issue a complete response letter that rejected that SNDA. A district court does not have jurisdiction to review such agency action. Jurisdiction over such action is vested by the FDCA exclusively in the appropriate court of appeals on a petition for review brought by the sponsor whose application was denied. *See* 21 U.S.C. § 355(h). The Court acknowledged this limitation on its subject matter jurisdiction, observing that "the only decision subject to review here is the denial of the Citizen Petition; I do not have any authority to review the denial of the

Plan B One–Step SNDA for the purpose of granting relief." *Tummino II*, 2013 WL 1348656, at *19.

That Citizen Petition did not request FDA action as to all "levonorgestrel-based emergency contraceptives" as the Court's remedy addresses. The Citizen Petition sought agency action only on Plan B (the original two-pill product) and its generic equivalents. *See* Admin. R. at CP 21 [Case No. 05-366] (requesting that "the Food and Drug Administration (FDA) switch from prescription to over-the-counter (OTC) status two FDA-approved emergency contraceptive drugs, Preven [which is no longer marketed] and Plan B, and any new drug eligible for filing an abbreviated new drug application because of its equivalence to" those drug products). The Court's determination that the agency's denial of the Citizen Petition was arbitrary and capricious could support relief only with regard to that agency action. Thus, the relief awarded must be limited to the specific products covered by the Citizen Petition and not to other products such as PBOS. But, the Court's Order authorizes FDA to comply with its injunction by lifting the restrictions on PBOS without making any change to the two-pill Plan B, as long as FDA "actually believes there is any significant difference between the one- and two-pill products." *Tummino II*, 2013 WL 1348656, at *31.

Moreover, the Court's decision undertakes an extensive review of Teva's February 2011 PBOS SNDA, the end result of which is an Order to FDA to reverse its December 2011 agency action and make available PBOS without a prescription or point-of-sale restriction to all ages. The Court first ordered FDA to "make levonorgestrel-based emergency contraceptives available without a prescription and without point-of-sale or age restrictions." *Id.* at *31. It then went on, however, to expressly preclude FDA from complying with this directive by means of "administrative rulemaking proceedings." *Id.* at *32. But FDA's regulations allow it to effect such a change from a prescription drug product to OTC in only two possible ways – by approving a drug sponsor's SNDA or through a notice-and-comment rulemaking proceeding (which may be initiated *sua sponte* by the Commissioner or in response to a citizen petition).[4] If the rulemaking option is foreclosed, as it is under the Court's Order, then the only available way for FDA to comply with the Court's directive is to request that Teva's submit an SNDA for PBOS seeking the same changes as the February 2011 SNDA, as to which FDA issued the complete response letter in December 2011, and to grant that SNDA. Thus, the Court essentially directs FDA to reverse its decision on Teva's February 2011 SNDA for PBOS, something the Court concededly lacks the power to do.

Thus, despite the Court's recognition that it does "not have any authority to review the denial of the [PBOS] SNDA for the purpose of granting relief," *id.* at *19, the relief it ultimately granted is precisely the change Teva had unsuccessfully sought in its February 2011 SNDA for PBOS. The Court therefore encroached upon the exclusive jurisdiction of the courts of appeals to review and provide relief with respect to SNDAs. *See Merritt v. Shuttle, Inc.*, 245 F.3d 182, 187 (2d Cir. 2001) ("statutes . . . that vest judicial review of administrative orders exclusively in the courts of appeals also preclude district courts from hearing claims that are 'inextricably intertwined' with review of such orders") (citation omitted); *see also FCC v. ITT World Communications Inc.*, 466

---

[4] The Court agreed in *Tummino I* that these were the only options available to FDA for achieving a change to a drug's prescription status. *Tummino v. Torti*, 603 F. Supp. 2d 519, 525 (E.D.N.Y. 2009) (*Tummino I*). The court held in its Order, however, "that no statute or regulation requires the FDA to engage in administrative rulemaking upon approval of a citizen petition or *sua sponte* reconsideration of a drug's prescription-only status." *Tummino II*, 2013 WL 1348656, at *32. The Court opined that 21 U.S.C. § 353(b)(3)'s language is permissive rather than mandatory, and that 21 C.F.R. § 10.30 allows FDA to change a drug's prescription status in response to a citizen petition by regulatory fiat without having to initiate a rulemaking proceeding. *Id.* Contrary to the Court's interpretation, however, the language in 21 C.F.R. § 10.30 does not expand the Commissioner's power or authorize her to take agency actions that she would not be authorized to take in contexts outside of a citizen petition, and it does not mean that a citizen petition authorizes the Commissioner to effect a change to OTC other than by rulemaking or by approval of an SNDA. It simply means that the Commissioner has the authority, in response to a citizen petition, to pursue an otherwise available course of agency action that is different from what the petition proposed. The Court's own decision in *Tummino I* supports at least a substantial possibility that the Court's construction of the regulation will be reversed on appeal. The Court should, in any event, have deferred to this reasonable interpretation by FDA of its own statute and regulations, which is supported by the plain language. *See Thomas Jefferson Univ. v. Shalala*, 512 U.S. 504, 512 (1994); *Martin v. Occupational Safety & Health Review Comm'n*, 499 U.S. 144, 150-151 (1991).

U.S. 463 (1984); *Telecommunications Research & Action Ctr. (TRAC) v. FCC*, 750 F.2d 70, 77 (D.C. Cir. 1984) (statutes that vest judicial review of administrative orders exclusively in the courts of appeals extend to "any suit seeking relief that *might* affect the Circuit Court's *future* jurisdiction") (emphasis added).

Because the Court articulated that it does not have jurisdiction to review – or, therefore, to order relief with respect to – PBOS, there clearly is at least a substantial possibility that the government will prevail on the appeal. Thus, the Court should stay its Order and judgment.

B.   **The Court Exceeded Its Authority In Ordering A Change for Plan B From Prescription To OTC Instead of Remanding to the Agency For Further Action.**

The remedy the Court ordered with respect to the levonorgestrel-based emergency contraceptives that was the actual subject of the Citizen Petition – the two-pill product Plan B – was also erroneous. And there is a substantial likelihood that the Court of Appeals will so rule because the specific relief this Court awarded – in the nature of a mandatory injunction directing FDA to approve all "levonorgestrel-based emergency contraceptives" for unrestricted OTC marketing within 30 days – exceeded the Court's authority.

Having found the agency's denial of the Citizen Petition to be arbitrary and capricious, the Court erred in ordering a circumvention of the administrative process, substituting its judgment for the agency's, and directing a specific substantive regulatory course of action. The relief directed by the Court is essentially in the nature of mandamus because it directs the outcome of how an agency is to exercise its authority, rather than directing the agency to exercise its authority in conformance with the law as stated by the Court. *See Norton v. So. Utah Wilderness Alliance (SUWA)*, 542 U.S. 55, 63-65 (2004). It is well-established, however, that mandamus is an "extraordinary remedy" that "will issue only to compel the performance of a clear and nondiscretionary duty." *Pittston Coal Group v. Sebben*, 488 U.S. 105, 121 (1988); *see also*

SUWA, 542 U.S. at 63; *Califano v. Yamasaki*, 442 U.S. 682, 698 (1979); *Association of Am. Med. Colleges v. Califano*, 569 F.2d 101, 111 n.80 (D.C. Cir. 1977) ("it is to be employed only under exceptional circumstances, for courts will intervene to disturb the determinations of administrative officers only in clear cases of illegality"). Moreover, even when mandamus is granted, courts are not to direct or influence the exercise of discretion of the officer or agency in the making of the decision. *See Wilbur v. United States*, 281 U.S. 206, 218 (1930) (a court cannot, pursuant to its mandamus jurisdiction, "direct the exercise of judgment or discretion in a particular way"); *SUWA*, 542 U.S. at 64; *United States ex rel. Schonbrun v. Commanding Officer, Armed Forces*, 403 F.2d 371, 374 (2d Cir. 1968); *see also Environmental Defense Fund*, 578 F.2d at 339 (courts must "proceed with particular caution, avoiding all temptation to direct the agency in a choice between rational alternatives."). The Court neither considered nor adhered to these precedents but instead granted a mandatory injunction that directed the exercise of judgment or discretion in a particular way.

Rather than issuing a directive to the agency as to what specific action to take, the Court should have remanded to the agency for compliance with its legal ruling. It is well-established that if the agency record does not support the action under review, if the agency did not consider all the relevant factors, if the agency did not furnish an adequate explanation for its decision, or if the reviewing court cannot evaluate the challenged agency action on the basis of the record before it, then

> the proper course, except in rare circumstances, is to remand to the agency for additional investigation or explanation. The reviewing court is not generally empowered to conduct a *de novo* inquiry into the matter being reviewed and to reach its own conclusions based on such an inquiry.

Florida Power & Light Co. v. Lorion, 470 U.S. 729, 744 (1985); *see also INS v. Ventura*, 537 U.S. 12, 16, 18 (2002); *Ethyl Corp. v. EPA*, 541 F.2d 1, 36 (D.C. Cir. 1976) (*en banc*).[5]   This Court acknowledged these principles in *Tummino I*, noting that: "When a court reviewing an agency decision rules in favor of the plaintiff, it generally remands to the agency rather than granting affirmative relief." *Tummino I*, 603 F. Supp. 2d at 549.   It went on to recognize a limited exception to this general remand rule in situations where the record has already been fully developed, and that remand would fail to serve any useful purpose; it however rejected plaintiffs' suggestion that that exception be applied in the case, both because the leadership of FDA "can be trusted to conduct a fair assessment of the scientific evidence" on remand and *also* because "a decision whether Plan B, a systemic hormonal contraceptive drug, may be used safely without a prescription by children as young as 11 or 12, is best left to the expertise of the FDA, to which Congress has entrusted this responsibility; it should not be made by a federal district court judge." *Id.* at 549.   Although the Court's latest opinion proceeds differently on the first aspect, the expertise of the agency in this area remains.

Here, the proper course of action should have been to remand for further agency consideration, or for elaboration of the basis for a decision not to proceed with rulemaking as to Plan B. The Court's Order interferes with and thereby undermines the regulatory procedures governing FDA's drug approval process. A drug approval decision involves scientific judgments as to whether statutory and regulatory factors are met that warrant deference to those charged with the statutory responsibility to make those decisions.   The agency alone has the necessary information and scientific expertise to assess the data and information required to make a determination that a drug is safe and effective.

---

[5] This principle is echoed in FDA's own regulations. *See* 21 C.F.R. § 10.45(i)(1), (2).

Nevertheless, the Court declined to remand to the agency. Instead, it stepped into FDA's shoes, directed the scientific conclusions that the agency must draw from the record before it, and granted relief beyond the scope of the Citizen Petition. It failed to cite to or distinguish *Lorion, Ethyl Corp.,* or their progeny, or to explain why a remand would fail to serve a useful purpose at this point.[6] Indeed, over the past eight years, FDA has invested thousands of hours reviewing and acting upon multiple iterations of SNDAs, generic competitors, as well as the Citizen Petition. On remand, FDA would reconsider, consistent with any governing legal ruling by the Court, the Citizen Petition regarding Plan B and its generics in light of the applicable scientific data or information. Thus, at a minimum, the government has a substantial possibility of success on the merits of this point on appeal, and a stay is appropriate.

II.   **A STAY WILL NOT HARM PLAINTIFFS.**

The plaintiffs – including the most recently added plaintiff – are all over age 15 and therefore will soon be able to obtain at least one emergency contraceptive containing levonorgestrel (*viz.*, PBOS) without a prescription at retail establishments that have a pharmacy counter. Thus, an injunction is not required to afford relief to any of the plaintiffs.[7] They can purchase the product whenever the store is open (regardless of whether the pharmacy is open) by showing proof of age.[8] Accordingly, all the plaintiffs in this case will soon have access to

---

[6] The one situation where *Tummino I* had recognized a limited exception to the general remand rule – where the record had already been fully developed, so that remand would fail to serve any useful purpose – clearly does not apply here, since the Court considered materials that had never been submitted to the Citizen Petition docket.

[7] Even assuming *arguendo* that Teva's previous point-of-sale restrictions could somehow have caused a justiciable injury-in-fact to any of the plaintiffs, its newly-approved amended SNDA largely dispenses with those restrictions in favor of a new point-of-sale regime proposed by Teva that is even less demanding of consumers. The Court has no evidence before it that any plaintiff will suffer injury-in-fact under this new regime; certainly, the specific point-of-sale restrictions that this Court found to potentially cause injury to some consumers of emergency contraceptives are no longer in place for PBOS.

[8] The requirement to show proof of age to purchase a product has been held not to impair a legally-protected interest. *See **Error! Main Document Only.***Whalen v. Roe*, 429 U.S. 589, 599, 601-02 (1977); *see also Immediato v. Rye Neck Sch. Dist.*, 73 F.3d 454, 463 (2d Cir. 1996); *Barry v. New York*, 712 F.2d 1554, 1559

levonorgestrel-containing emergency contraceptives without meaningful restrictions or impediments. Therefore, no plaintiff has a basis to assert harm from a stay of the Court's Order and judgment pending appeal.

This is, moreover, not a class action, so the extraordinary relief the Court ordered – directing FDA to make PBOS available OTC without restriction despite its lack of jurisdiction over FDA's decision concerning that drug, and directing FDA to dispense with rulemaking required by the regulatory framework to provide for public participation and instead to take immediate substantive action for Plan B – cannot be justified on the ground that Plan B or PBOS should be made available to others. In the exercise of its equitable power in a suit under the APA, a court must confine its remedy to redressing the injury asserted by the parties before the Court. *See Monsanto Co. v. Geertson Seed Farms*, 130 S.Ct. 2743, 2761 (2010).

III.   DEFENDANTS AND THE PUBLIC INTEREST WILL SUFFER IRREPARABLE HARM ABSENT A STAY.

As set forth above, under Second Circuit precedent, the degree of irreparable injury that a movant must demonstrate to support a stay pending appeal is inversely proportional to the degree of probability of success on the merits of the appeal. *Mohammed*, 309 F.3d at 101. Because the government has demonstrated above a very substantial likelihood of success on appeal, the degree of irreparable injury it must demonstrate is reduced. That standard is readily met here because, absent a stay, the Court's decision will cause irreparable harm to the government, and to the public it serves.

FDA and the public would be irreparably and immediately harmed if a drug product that purported to be "FDA approved" were approved instead at the direction of a court. The public properly relies upon FDA classification of drugs as non-prescription as a reflection of the agency's judgment regarding the safety and proper use of a drug without a doctor's prescription. Thus, the

---

(2d Cir. 1983).

public interest will not be served by reclassification of drugs as non-prescription without agency approval. A stay of the Court's Order will prevent public uncertainty regarding the status of the drugs at issue here pending the government's appeal to the Second Circuit. Moreover, if the status of these drugs is changed and later reversed, it can lead to situations in which women mistakenly believe that they can obtain the drug without a prescription or at certain locations where it used to be available, but is no longer.

Further, FDA has long interpreted its regulations to provide that the agency cannot effect a change from prescription to OTC by simply granting a Citizen Petition. A change to OTC requires either the drug sponsor to submit an SNDA with supporting data or else the agency to conduct notice-and-comment rulemaking in which all interested members of the public — not only those who filed a Citizen Petition — may participate and assist in developing a complete record on which the agency can then base its expert decision. Permitting a member of the public to seek to alter the indication of an approved drug product by filing a petition, as the Court seems to do, would undermine the separate regulatory proceedings of citizen petitions and drug applications, interfere with proprietary interests drug companies have in their NDAs, and significantly weaken the incentives for drug innovators to invest in drug development, including seeking new indications. Because such a ruling would harm the public, the public interest favors a stay.

A.   **Failure to Grant a Stay Will Result in Substantial Market Confusion, Irreparably Harming FDA's and the Public's Interest in the Orderly Functioning of the Drug Regulatory System.**

If FDA were required to comply with the Court's Order pending appeal, at least some emergency contraceptive drug products containing levonorgestrel would become available to all ages without a prescription or point-of-sale or labeling restrictions. If the Court's Order were to be found on appeal to be in excess of the Court's authority (which there is a substantial probability of, for the reasons set forth above), FDA would take appropriate action to withdraw the unrestricted OTC approval and to reinstate the product's previous approval status. Such a rescission can reasonably be expected to cause substantial market confusion, harming FDA's and the public's interest in the orderly functioning of the drug regulatory system.

For example, now that PBOS is approved for OTC availability with a labeling restriction that the product is not for sale to consumers under age 15, and with a requirement of age verification by retail cashiers, retailers will train their employees on how the product may now be sold. Absent a stay, if FDA were required to approve the marketing of PBOS to women of all ages during the pendency of an appeal, those retailers would need to instruct their employees to make the product available without any age verification. If the Court Order were then to be vacated, the retailers would again need to instruct and retrain their employees as to how to re-impose the age restriction. The likely confusion of retail employees will only exacerbate consumer confusion as to the availability of PBOS.

In addition, if the Second Circuit vacates this Court's Order, the products held for unrestricted sale at the time the appeal is decided would be misbranded under the FDCA, 21 U.S.C. § 352. It is likely that the misbranded version of the product (*i.e.*, labeled for unrestricted OTC use) would exist alongside properly labeled versions of the product (labeled for OTC use only in women down to age 15) during a potentially extended transitional period while retailers clear their inventory and replenish their stocks. This circumstance would also confuse and thereby irreparably harm consumers.

B.   The Government's Interest in Conferring Marketing Exclusivity Will Be Irreparably Harmed Absent a Stay.

Congress provided marketing exclusivity periods in the FDCA to encourage the development of new and improved drugs, thereby protecting and promoting the public health.

The FDCA provides that, when a drug sponsor invests funds to conduct or sponsor new clinical studies that FDA finds are essential to the approval of an SNDA, FDA is to grant three years of exclusivity with respect to the change approved in the SNDA. *See* 21 U.S.C. §§ 355(c)(3)(E)(iv), 355(j)(5)(E)(iv); 21 C.F.R. § 314.108(b)(5). This exclusivity bars FDA from approving that same change for a generic version of the drug for three years. Congress intended this exclusivity to provide an economic incentive for pioneer companies to engage in the expensive clinical research necessary to support the approval of significant changes to a drug's approval status, such as approval for use in new patient populations. *See AstraZeneca Pharm. v. FDA*, 872 F. Supp. 2d 60, 89-90 (D.D.C. 2012).

It is undisputed that, based on FDA's representations regarding the need for additional data to support approving PBOS for use without a prescription by younger age groups, Teva conducted actual use studies that included participation by sufficient numbers of 15 and 16 year olds. The agency deemed those studies essential to approval of non-prescription use of the drug by those age groups. The Court nevertheless implies in its decision that FDA cannot grant Teva marketing exclusivity for a change for PBOS from prescription to OTC simply because FDA issued a complete response letter to Teva in December 2011 and Teva chose not to file a petition for review to the court of appeals. This implication ignored the prospect that, instead of appealing, Teva could file an amended SNDA, which FDA could approve, leading to a grant of exclusivity. That is what happened when FDA recently approved Teva's 15-and-up amended SNDA and gave Teva three years of marketing exclusivity for the newly approved use.

To the extent the Court's decision can be read to deprive Teva marketing exclusivity under the circumstances here – that is, to the extent it can be read to require FDA to also approve generic versions of PBOS for nonprescription use without age restrictions – it will cause irreparable harm to the regulatory process by undermining the benefits to the public and to FDA of the marketing exclusivity that the FDCA affords to drug sponsors. As noted, such exclusivity provides a critical incentive for drug development that advances FDA's goal of protecting and promoting public health. To the extent the Court's order is construed to eliminate Teva's entitlement to exclusivity, it undermines the incentive for drug companies to conduct new clinical research studies to support new uses or indications, because it permits competitors to take advantage of the investments of market innovators free of charge. Such a result would stifle rather than encourage innovation, to the detriment of the public.

CONCLUSION

For the foregoing reasons, defendants respectfully request a stay pending appeal. If this Court is not inclined to grant a stay pending appeal, defendants respectfully respect that the Court enter a temporary administrative stay of the Court's Order and judgment pending resolution by the Court of Appeals of any motion defendants might make to that court under FRAP 8(a)(2).

Dated: May 1, 2013   Respectfully submitted,

STUART F. DELERY   LORETTA E. LYNCH
Acting Assistant Attorney General   United States Attorney
Civil Division   Eastern District of New York
                                   271 Cadman Plaza East
IAN HEATH GERSHENGORN   Brooklyn, NY 11201-1820
Deputy Assistant Attorney General

SHEILA LIEBER   By: /s/ {FILED ELECTRONICALLY}
Deputy Director,   F. FRANKLIN AMANAT (FA6117)
Federal Programs Branch   Assistant United States Attorney
                                   Eastern District of New York
ERIC B. BECKENHAUER   (718) 254-6024
Trial Attorney,   franklin.amanat@usdoj.gov
Federal Programs Branch
United States Department of Justice, Civil Division
20 Massachusetts Avenue, N.W.
Washington, DC 20530
(202) 514-3338

Of Counsel:

DAVID J. HOROWITZ, Deputy General Counsel
ELIZABETH H. DICKINSON, Chief Counsel, Food and Drug Division
ANNAMARIE KEMPIC, Deputy Chief Counsel, Litigation, Food and Drug Division
SCOTT A. KAPLAN, Assistant Chief Counsel, Food and Drug Division
United States Department of Health and Human Services
Office of the General Counsel
10903 New Hampshire Avenue
Silver Spring, MD 20993-0002

Appendix D: Administrative Advocacy Checklist

Best Practices in Administrative Proceedings

Overview

- Administrative proceedings are only vaguely similar to standard civil trials. Both are governed by due process considerations, but practice and procedures differ.
- The degree of formality varies widely among administrative agencies and administrative bench officers, so your presentation must be flexibly tailored to each forum.
- Present all of the issues and evidence (testimonial, documentary, demonstrative) to address the statute, rules, and regulations requirements.

Checklist: Preparing for Hearing

Know the Agency's Process

- ☐ Review the enabling statute that creates an agency or accords it power. This might provide specific administrative procedural guidance for agency hearings.
- ☐ Study the agency's procedural regulations, rulings, policy manuals, or internal operating procedures governing hearings.

Note

If the agency has not adopted procedural rules or its procedural rules are limited, review the model rules in your state, generally found in the state Model Administrative Procedure Act.

- ☐ Consider due process requirements under the U.S. Constitution.
- ☐ Drafting a basic outline for a brief before the hearing is useful to get organized and really understand the case.

Know Your Presiding Officer

☐ Determine whether the administrative judge is assigned to the agency by the Office of Administrative Hearing or employed by the agency.

☐ Review similar subject-matter decisions by the administrative judge, if possible.

☐ Gather information from other advocates about the particular practices of the administrative officer before whom you will appear.

- Does the judge play an active role in testimony?
- How are exhibits handled?
- Are any evidentiary rules in play?
- How does the judge treat participants?
- Is the judge formal, or are participants allowed lots of leeway?
- Does the hearing officer have unusual quirks?

Physical Layout Challenges

☐ Administrative hearings are held in a variety of settings, often informal, such as meeting and conference rooms.

☐ Consider visiting the hearing room in advance to see where the presiding officer sits, the physical layout for you and your client, and where witnesses and staff sit in relation to the judge.

☐ Most hearings are open to the public, but the hearing officer may issue an order excluding witnesses.

☐ Confirm availability of easel, computer, monitor, electrical outlets, and so on.

☐ Determine how the record is going to be preserved. Consider buying the transcript or making your own recording (either by tape or reporter) if you anticipate the need for citations in posthearing briefs or if you anticipate the need to appeal.

Prehearing Considerations

Discovery

☐ Discovery may be entirely prohibited or limited.

☐ Except as otherwise provided by agency rules, the presiding officer has broad discretion to decide whether and how much discovery to permit.

☐ The administrative judge may entertain (though not necessarily grant) requests to permit depositions, requests for admissions, and all other procedures authorized in civil discovery.

☐ For subpoenas of witnesses and records seeking information through third parties, the presiding officer will consider the following:

- Whether all parties are represented by counsel
- Whether undue expense or delay in bringing the case to hearing will result

- Whether the discovery will promote the orderly and prompt conduct of the proceeding
- Whether the interests of justice will be promoted

☐ Start with informal (letter) discovery by communicating with other parties about facts, documents, and public records.

☐ Freedom of Information Act Requests include the following:

- Are an effective means of discovery unique to administrative law
- Can be used to request agency documents, instead of engaging in formal discovery, or as a supplement
- Can result in disclosure of documents submitted to the agency during administrative litigation similar to your case
- Can include internal e-mails, memoranda, or interpretive statements on how the agency implements a statute or regulation

Note

In most cases, protocol is to copy the other parties and the administrative bench officer's clerk before making a public records request. Requests should be descriptive, so as not to accidentally exclude what you need, but tailored narrowly to avoid a scatter-shot approach, which can alienate agency staff.

Hearing Practice
Opening Statements

☐ Anticipate opening comments by the presiding officer, possibly outlining issues the administrative judge believes need to be addressed.

☐ Before the hearing and off the record, seek permission from the administrative judge to make an opening statement.

☐ Succinctly state your theory of the case. Highlight the most important evidence that supports your theory. Clearly state what you are asking for (the focused ask).

☐ Pretend you are at a party telling a stranger your case. Practice communicating the issues and summarizing the evidence. Listen to and seriously consider the feedback you get.

Note

Don't bother practicing with people who will tell you you're great. This is a waste of time. Seek out listeners with the intellectual discipline to listen critically and give painfully honest feedback.

☐ Keep it short and simple. If your case has complicated aspects to it and you need more than a few minutes, submit a prehearing memorandum. Consider using a timeline (yes, from fourth grade), graphs, charts, or other graphics that communicate extensive information in compressed formats.

Direct Examination

☐ The goal of direct examination is to prove a prima facie case. It is the key to developing a complete record; be sure to cover all essential facts and law.

☐ If certain facts help the administrative judge find in your favor, touch on them in direct examination.

☐ Prepare witnesses to present testimony in a simple, direct, orderly, coherent manner. Never let them ramble.

☐ Consider using prefiled testimony (affidavits, depositions, reports, statements, prior testimony) to support or enhance live direct examination.

☐ Prepare your direct examination so that witness testimony begins and ends on strong points (an exception to presenting facts chronologically).

☐ Do not state facts yourself; do not express opinions about witness testimony while examining the witness. Closing argument is the time to address credibility and weight.

Caveat

Be cognizant of the hearing record, in whatever form (written, recorded, transcribed, dictated). Many administrative agency decisions are decided on appeal. Be sure your objections and evidence are captured and clearly reflected in the record.

Role of the Presiding Officer

☐ The administrative bench officer may conduct an initial examination of witnesses before your direct examination.

☐ Do not treat the administrative bench officer as an adverse party. If his or her questions seem objectionable, consider the costs and benefits of objecting to the administrative bench officer about the administrative bench officer.

☐ If an objection is necessary to protect appeal rights, object and succinctly state your reasons for objecting. Make sure your objection is captured on the record.

☐ Follow the administrative bench officer's question set (if any) with your own questions.

Caveat
During your presentation, be alert for indications that the administrative bench officer does not understand you or the witness, so you can clarify the confusion immediately.

Caveat
Ex parte communication is prohibited. If you have any doubt about whether your procedural question is problematic, send your query by e-mail to the administrative bench officer's clerk and copy opposing counsel.

Cross-Examination

- ☐ Consider your opponent's probable theory of the case; prepare cross-examination questions for each opposition witness.
- ☐ To control an adverse witness during cross-examination, avoid open-ended questions. Prepare questions requiring only "yes" or "no" answers.
- ☐ If the witness evades a question, simply repeat the question politely until you get an answer; or ask the administrative bench officer to instruct the witness to answer the question; or reply with, "That sounds like a 'Yes' (or a 'No'), is that correct?"
- ☐ Questions should progress logically toward a specific goal. Each question should introduce only one new fact.

Caveat
Do not argue with the witness.

- ☐ Wait until the hearing to decide whether to cross-examine a particular witness (but prepare carefully, just the same).
- ☐ If your case is strong, minimize your risks; do not cross-examine.

Consider forgoing cross-examination:

- ☐ If the witness did not hurt the essential elements of your case or if the witness' testimony was not credible.

☐ If the witness failed to bring up damaging testimony on direct, avoid opening the door by raising the topic on cross-examination (which would create a second chance to raise the damaging testimony on opposing counsel's redirect).

☐ If the facts of your case could go either way, consider whether to ask the witness a question that you do not know the answer to, or take other risks on cross-examination.

Redirect Examination

☐ Redirect is appropriate to correct misstatements, inconsistencies, or misleading impressions that may have been created during cross-examination. For this reason, redirect examination should be focused on what is necessary to correct a witness' testimony, rehabilitate a witness' credibility, and clarify a witness' favorable testimony.

☐ Ask the administrative bench officer for the opportunity to reexamine your witnesses after your opponent or the administrative bench officer has questioned them.

Closing

☐ Closing argument practice varies according to the type of hearing and the style of the administrative bench officer.

☐ Ask the administrative bench officer before the hearing starts whether closing arguments will be permitted and, if so, whether orally or in writing, or both; ask about rebuttal after your opponent's closing argument (the administrative bench officer may require you to reserve time from your closing, if time limits are in force).

☐ Give a short, persuasive oral closing argument; give a detailed summary of the facts and the law in your posthearing brief.

Evidentiary Matters
Rules of Evidence

☐ Administrative hearings are typically less formal than standard civil court proceedings; any evidence that a reasonably prudent person would rely on will probably be admitted.

☐ Hearsay is (generally) admissible, but (usually) it cannot be the sole basis of the administrative bench officer's decision, so plan to supplement it with other evidence that is not hearsay.

☐ Rules of evidence may apply by analogy or reference as a guide, to the extent the administrative bench officer determines, taking into account constitutional due process requirements.

Objections

☐ Before the hearing, consider the evidence you will introduce, anticipate possible objections, and prepare justifications for admission on evidentiary grounds.

☐ Consider the evidence that your opponent is likely to introduce, whether you may have a sound basis for objecting to its admission, and how and when you must object to preserve the record for appeal.

☐ If the administrative bench officer overrules your objections, offer to submit a posthearing brief to preserve the issue for appeal instead of arguing the point at the hearing, at the risk of alienating the administrative bench officer.

☐ Use objections sparingly (mostly to make a record for appeal). Instead of objecting, make note of hearsay, irrelevance, and other evidentiary weaknesses; emphasize them in closing or posthearing briefs.

Use of Exhibits

☐ The procedure for introducing exhibits at an administrative hearing is less formal than in standard civil trial proceedings, but be prepared to lay a proper foundation (who prepared the document, when, and why? Where was the document found?).

☐ Depending on the type of case, submitting exhibits and documents to the administrative bench officer before going on the record before the hearing may be preferable.

☐ Some administrative agency rules contain protocols for submitting documentary evidence and may even prescribe exhibit numbering or formatting standards; be sure you check the rules and comply with them.

☐ Admitting all documents and other evidence before going on the record is not a problem if you are merely stipulating to the admissibility of unobjectionable documents. But insist that any objections to the admissibility of a document take place on the record.

☐ Be sure that the way the exhibits come into evidence ensures that the administrative bench officer and any appellate tribunal understand the purpose, nature, authenticity, and reliability of each exhibit.

☐ Before the hearing, prepare an index of the evidence you need to have admitted (in a document on your laptop or in a binder) with numbered exhibits, and check off each item as it is admitted (this job is often delegated to the client). See Appendix A.

Posthearing Concerns
Leaving the Record Open

☐ Check the applicable regulations to determine whether posthearing submissions are permitted and, if so, what procedures you must follow.

☐ You may ask to keep the record open for a defined period to submit additional evidence or posthearing memoranda, particularly if problematic issues surfaced at the hearing.

☐ If the administrative bench officer leaves the record open for the submission of additional evidence, obtain that evidence, and submit it as quickly as possible; doublecheck that it has been received (do this even if you get a signed return receipt postcard or confirmation that an e-mail was opened).

Posthearing Briefing

☐ In most administrative hearing settings, you have the right to file a posthearing memorandum after the hearing concludes.

☐ The advantage of submitting a posthearing briefing is that you can incorporate the actual testimony and evidence that was presented, which can be particularly important if the opposition introduced evidence that surprised you or requires explanation or analysis.

☐ Administrative decisions sometimes closely parallel well-written hearing briefs. Boost your case by submitting a brief that can be easily cut and pasted into a decision and order (submit both PDF and Word document formats).

Appendix E: Legal Research Guide to Administrative Law

The United States Government Manual (found online at https://www.usgovern mentmanual.gov/) lists every U.S. administrative agency and its functions, as well as citations to the enabling statute for each agency. The manual contains a subject index to help locate agencies that regulate a particular area of law. Once you have the citation to the enabling statute, you can look it up in an annotated code volume (found online at https://www.gpo.gov/fdsys/browse/collectionUScode. action?collectionCode=USCODE; see "Statutes") to find the legislation itself, as well as references to relevant primary (cases and statutes) and secondary source (articles analyzing the topic, citing to cases) materials.

Finding Regulations

Administrative agencies create regulations (also called rules) that function like legislation. Regulations are published both chronologically and by subject. The chronological arrangement of regulations is found in the Federal Register, which is available free at https://www.federalregister.gov/ and at HeinOnline (found online at https://home.heinonline.org/titles/Federal-Register-Library–Code-of-Federal-Regulations/The-Federal-Register/?letter=T) and Bloomberg Law (from the "Legislative & Regulatory" tab, found online at https://www.bna.com/regulatory-search/).

Under the terms of the Administrative Procedure Act (5 U.S.C. 500 et seq., found online at https://www.archives.gov/federal-register/laws/administrative-procedure), agencies must first give notice of proposed rule making by publication in the Federal Register, along with a period during which interested parties may submit comments to the agency and recommend changes to the text of the proposed rule. After the comment period expires, the final rule is then published in the Federal Register, along with its effective date. In each proposed and final rule published in the Federal Register, there is a Supplementary Information section that explains the purpose of the rule, and in the case of a final rule, summaries of comments received during the comment period that indicate any changes that were made.

In addition to proposed and final rules, the Federal Register contains agency notices, presidential documents, notices of licenses issued, "Sunshine Act" meetings (under the government in the Sunshine Act, 5 U.S.C. 552b, "every portion of every meeting of an agency" must be open to "public observation"; found online at https://www.gpo.gov/fdsys/granule/USCODE-2011-title5/USCODE-2011-title5-partI-chap5-subchapII-sec552b; exceptions: matters of national security, the Central Intelligence Agency), and the "Current Unified Agenda of Regulatory and Deregulatory Actions"; found online at https://www.reginfo.gov/public/do /eAgendaMain, which is issued twice a year and summarizes the rules and proposed rules that each agency expects to issue during the year).

Efficient research of regulations in a chronologically arranged publication, without subject-area guidance, is impossible. To effectively research administrative law by subject or topic, use the Code of Federal Regulations (CFR), in print at most libraries and available as noncirculating reference material, and available free online at https://www.ecfr.gov/cgi-bin/text-idx?SID=bfbc647c49d11d3eb942 9916a0d7fbee&mc=true&node=se2.1.25_1100&rgn=div8.

The CFR is divided into Titles that group material on the same subject in the same place. The CFR is divided into 50 titles; titles do not always match their USC title counterparts. Each CFR title is divided into Parts (major subdivisions); Parts are divided into Sections.

Using an index is the best way to access the CFR. Regulatory language is often highly technical and scientific, and without knowing the precise terms used by the agency, finding rules through keyword searching can be very challenging. For a good print index to the CFR, the United States Code Service (USCS) "Index and Finding Aids to Code of Federal Regulations" volume at the end of the USCS set is more user-friendly than the CFR index.

Updating Regulations

After finding the text of the regulations in the CFR that you are interested in, you must update your research. Regulations are constantly amended, and thorough research requires review of court decisions interpreting or overruling regulations. The CFR publication updates occur quarterly:

Titles 1 through 16: updated January 1
Titles 17 through 27: updated April 1
Titles 28 through 41: updated July 1
Titles 42 through 50: updated October 1

Note

The color of the CFR volumes changes each year, so the print CFR volumes on the shelf will always be different colors (because of the rolling update publication schedule) yet entirely current.

You can check for updates to the text of a CFR section by checking the CFR's List of Sections Affected (LSA, available online at https://www.gpo.gov/fdsys/browse/collection.action?collectionCode=LSA), a monthly cumulative publication that lists proposed, new, and amended federal regulations that have been published in the Federal Register since the most recent revision date of a CFR title.

Each LSA issue is cumulative and contains the CFR part and section numbers, a description of its status (e.g., amended, confirmed, revised), and the Federal Register page number where the change(s) may be found.

How to use the LSA online:

Check the date of the CFR volume that contains your regulation to determine the date from which you need to update.

On the LSA page online, click on the most recent year, then the most recent month.

Find the CFR Title you are researching in, then open the PDF file. If there are changes to your section, you will see a reference to the Federal Register where the change occurred.

Go back to the Federal Register page online and open today's Federal Register. At the back, you'll see a List of CFR Parts Affected that is cumulative for the current month. Check to see whether your CFR section/part has been updated during the month. Depending on the date, you may have to check the same list from the last Federal Register of the prior month for any changes.

Alternatively, you can use the e-CFR (found online at https://ecfr.io/), a regularly updated, unofficial, nonlegal edition of the CFR. The benefit of the e-CFR is that, like Bloomberg Law, it incorporates changes to the text much more quickly than the official version of the CFR, and is free. The downside is that, like Bloomberg, it is not official, so you'll want to doublecheck to make sure you did not miss any changes. If you see any citations to Federal Register pages at the end of a CFR section in the e-CFR or Bloomberg Law, you can use those to double-check the changes and make sure the text is correct. Be sure to check the "Data is current as of" date on the e-CFR's main page; if not today's date, you need to manually check for updates.

The final step in updating is to make sure that you have found any judicial decisions that have applied, interpreted, or negatively treated your CFR section. No version of the CFR is annotated with case law, so you need to separately check for cases discussing your regulation.

Table of Cases

Glossary

NOTE *These references often arise in administrative law settings and can help practitioners decipher agency government-speak.*

~Numeric Designations~

§ 527 Organization   A tax-exempt group organized under § 527 of the U.S. tax code; § 527 organizations may not advocate for or against a particular candidate but may raise money for issue advocacy.

~A~

Abuse of Discretion, Reasonableness   Under the federal Administrative Procedure Act (APA), abuse of discretion is one element used in describing the scope of judicial review. An administrative bench officer abuses discretion if no facts support the decision or the decision is the result of an irrational decisional calculus. Use of discretion should include an explanation to show reasonableness related to the language of the enabling statute; absent this explanation, the administrative bench officer's decision might be considered an abuse of discretion or irrational on review.

Act   A bill passed by the legislature and approved by the president or governor.

Action   The adoption or amendment (of a new rule with a new rule number) or repeal of a rule. Disposition of any question before a legislature.

Adjudication, Formal   Adversarial hearing, allowed by statute, as part of an administrative agency's decision process; specific procedures are usually prescribed by the federal or state Administrative Procedure Act (the APA).

Adjudication, Informal   Agency decision made without formal adversarial procedures (such as trials), relying on inspections, meetings, and negotiations; made by the agency head or designee. Administrative process or agency action that does not involve formal adjudication or rule making; most agency decisions are informal, not formal.

Administrative Agency, Commission, Corporation, Board, Department, Division   A government body with authority to implement legislation.

Administrative Law   Branch of law governing the creation and operation of government agencies; focused on the powers granted to government agencies, the substantive rules that agencies make, and the legal relationships between agencies and the public; the body of law created by government agencies and departments of the government that carry out the laws passed by Congress or state legislatures. When the government passes laws on a complicated issue, it sometimes needs help parsing the details of how the law will be implemented and enforced. Agencies fill in the gaps for the government and pass rules and regulations to achieve Congress' goals; this creates administrative law.

Administrative Law Judge, ALJ A bench officer who hears cases solely related to one agency's regulations (for example, Social Security benefits appeals); trier of fact who presides over administrative tribunals and adjudicates claims involving administrative law.

Administrative Procedure Act, APA A federal law establishing the rules and regulations for applications, claims, hearings, and appeals involving government agencies, including procedural formalities that agencies must use when making decisions and conducting judicial review of administrative agency decisions. A federal law governing how administrative agencies propose, enact, and enforce regulations. All 50 states have similar acts spelling out the rules for dealing with state government agencies.

Administrative Procedure Act Hearing, APA Hearings APAs usually set out the requirements for informal or notice and comment rule making, and formal adjudication hearings; the Model State APAs describe several types of adjudications.

Administrative Process Procedures used by administrative agencies, including subpoena power to ensure appearance of witnesses.

Adopt, Adoption Take final action to create, change, or repeal a regulation; approval of motions, amendments, or resolutions.

Adoption by Agency The date an administrative agency takes final action on a regulation.

Adversarial System System of law in which an issue is argued in court by opposing sides; commonly found in administrative law formal adjudications.

Agency A governmental regulatory body established by the legislature, with the power to create, monitor, and enforce specific regulations.

Agency Action Work of a governmental agency, including rule making, adjudication, enforcement of specific regulatory schemes.

Agency Files A source of evidence, when agencies are not bound to make decisions based on a closed record; if a closed record decision is required, use of evidence from agency files is prohibited; if a party needs evidence from an agency file, the record must be reopened, with notice and opportunity for comment provided to all parties.

Agency Informal Advice The public sometimes requests information from administrative agencies about a specific matter, because statutes and regulations are often confusingly broad and technical; this advice is not binding on an agency.

Agency Review of ALJ Adjudication Generally, agencies have internal appellate procedures to decide internal appeals; once internal agency appeals are exhausted, parties may have a right to appeal in state or federal courts. Agency decisions in an adjudication are based on the whole record, including the administrative bench officer's decision; agencies have de novo decision-making authority after the administrative bench officer's decision. The APA usually provides that parties can comment on an administrative bench officer's decision; comments may be written or oral, depending on the agency's procedural rules.

Agency Rules The manner in which agencies manage their internal processes; guidance regarding how situations are handled. The rules touch on all aspects of administrative proceedings, including rule making and adjudication.

ALJ Decision Administrative agency's intermediate report or preliminary decision; the administrative bench officer's decision may be the agency's final action because the parties cannot or do not get the agency head to review it and do not take the matter to a civil court for judicial review.

ALJ Disqualification, Motion to Disqualify ALJ   Bases include prejudice or partiality with respect to any party or an interest in the matter, or unpermitted ex parte contact; disqualification motions must be raised at the hearing; the administrative bench officer then rules on them. An administrative bench officer's decision on disqualification is not immediately appealable; the hearing will go on (the agency head reviews the ruling later).

Alternative Dispute Resolution by Administrative Agencies, ADR   Known as regulatory negotiation ("reg-neg"); the agency gathers parties or their representatives to try to reach consensus about proposed rules, so that the parties do not challenge the subsequently enacted regulation in court; reg-neg is not a substitute for formal hearings (ADR techniques are becoming more popular in administrative law).

APA Rule-Making Procedures   Guidance outlines in the Administrative Procedure Act that requires agencies, when adopting regulations, to give public notice, receive and consider public comments, submit their regulations and supporting rule-making files for review, and publish the regulations.

Appeal   Procedure for challenging decisions of a presiding official.

Archives   Public records kept by the secretary of state, including copies of all measures considered at each legislative session, journals, committee reports, and documents of historic value.

Attorney General Opinion   Some statutes allow individuals to submit questions to the attorney general's office seeking legal advice or analysis with regard to an administrative agency or regulation.

Author   Member of the legislature who introduces a legislative measure.

Authority of ALJ   The administrative bench officer has authority to run all aspects of the prehearing conference and the subsequent formal adjudication hearing. The administrative bench officer must make a complete record, rule on motions, and make the first-level agency decision based on that record.

~B~

Benefit-Cost Analysis   Listing all costs and all benefits associated with a proposed regulation; the sum of anticipated benefits should outweigh the sum of its present/future costs.

Benign Neglect   A "do nothing" approach based on a belief that, over time, the policy will improve, or at least not harm, the interests of the neglected group; a laissez-faire policy.

Bias   Prejudice in favor of a thing, person, or group compared with another; considered unfair.

Bias, ALJ vs. Agency   The decision maker may be disqualified where prejudicial bias is present. However, the agency head must run the agency, which involves the agency head in the matter before the final decision. The administrative bench officer may have no statutory duties other than running the hearing and writing the decision.

Bias topics, ALJ   Bias claims may involve issues of fact, law, policy, financial interest, or personal interest. Bias involving financial or personal interest is most likely to lead to disqualification of an administrative bench officer; it is of most concern where the decision must be based on a closed record created by an adversarial hearing process. Bias must generally be demonstrated through specific facts/instances, rather than a general atmosphere of distrust; substantial prejudice must be shown to have resulted from the alleged bias.

Bill   A proposed law introduced by a member of a legislature; if approved at all stages, it becomes a law.

Bill of Rights   The first 10 Amendments to the U.S. Constitution.

Blue Pencil (California)   The state Constitution grants the governor "line item veto" authority to reduce or eliminate any item of appropriation from any bill, including the Budget Bill; in the 1960s, the governor used a blue editor's pencil (see also, line item veto).

Burden of Proof   The burden of proof is on the proponent of a position. The burden of proof for agency-level decision making is generally preponderance of the evidence (the agency-level burden of proof is not the same as the judicial scope of review test, which is usually the substantial evidence test).

~C~

California Code of Regulations, CCR   Official compilation of regulations adopted by state agencies; the official source for state administrative law.

Central Panel   An effort to eliminate bias by administrative judges. Administrative judges are employed by a separate agency that assigns them out to other agencies, as needed. This contrasts with systems where the judge is an employee of the agency that makes the final decision and where the judge may be subject to the same pressures as other employees.

Change of Policy, Consistency   Agencies usually have a legislative, statutory delegation of authority sufficient to permit changes to policies; agencies must follow their own legislative rules until they are changed by new legislative rule making. In rule making, a new rule usually means a change of policy, and agencies must meet statutory requirements to justify the promulgation of a new rule. In adjudication, agencies may be required by case law or the APA to provide reasons for changes in policy; absent an explanation, courts may remand the decision to the agency.

Code(s)   Compilation of administrative laws, organized by subject matter.

Code of Federal Regulations, CFR   Yearly federal government series of books that includes all rules/regulations passed by administrative agencies.

Codifier of Rules   The chief administrative law judge or designee.

Collateral Estoppel   Doctrine that bars issues that have been litigated from being litigated again.

Combination of Functions, Deciding and Investigating   In formal adjudication, agency decisions must be based on a closed record, but the deciding official's judgment may not be affected by outside-the-record influences. This can be a problem for the agency when it engages in a combination of the investigation and decision functions.

Common Law   Law flowing from judicial rulings in court (not from statutes or the Constitution); it is controlling unless it conflicts with statutory law.

~D~

Declaratory Order, Administrative Agency   Individuals may request a formal answer from an agency in response to a specific, written question; agencies usually have discretion on whether to respond. If the agency responds, it is usually bound by its response on that specific situation.

Declaratory Order, Court   Order of a court that clarifies rights between parties where there is uncertainty. Individuals may seek declaratory orders from a court about an agency to clarify the law.

Delegated Authority, Delegation of Authority   Power granted by the legislature to administrative agencies to implement or enforce a statute, including the power to adopt regulations. Agencies can act only within the delegation in its statute; the statute determines whether the agency has formal adjudication or legislative rule-making authority. The agency must define its view of its delegation in the first instance; courts are deferential to agency interpretation. The court is least likely to be deferential when the statute is clear on its face or the statute uses nontechnical language familiar to the court, in which case, the court may substitute its interpretation where the agency has reached a contrary interpretation.

Delegation   Direction from the legislature to administrative agencies allowing them to administer their enabling statute or make decisions; administrative agencies can sometimes assign (delegate) their functions or powers.

Differs Substantially   Term describing the situation when a rule does one or more of the following: affects the interests of people who, based on the proposed text of the rule, could not reasonably have determined that the rule would affect their interests; addresses subject matter or an issue that is not addressed in the proposed text of the rule; or produces an effect that could not reasonably have been expected based on the proposed text of the rule.

Discretion   Discretion is inherent in agency action (or inaction). If no law applies, the exercise of discretion is not subject to judicial review. Courts defer to agency discretion in many decisions. Statutes may commit action to agency discretion. Choosing among reasonable choices, the decision to respond to requests for information, and the choice of rule making or adjudication as the vehicle to promulgate policy can all be discretionary. If the enabling statute is not clear on its face, its interpretation may be left to the discretion of the agency. Exercise of discretion must not be an abuse of discretion or unreasonable. Agencies have broad prosecutorial discretion.

Due Process   Individuals usually have a right to a hearing before an agency can act; at a minimum, the hearing must offer notice of the allegations and an opportunity to be heard in response. Something less than a full evidentiary hearing is required and some degree of error is acceptable. The opportunity to respond can be entirely in writing.

Due Process Hearing   After the determination of the existence of a protected interest, what procedure is adequate must then be determined; no single procedure covers all due process situations. The goal is to protect individuals from the mistaken or unjustified deprivation of life, liberty, or property. It allows individuals to contest the basis on which the government proposes to deprive them of protected interests (see *Mathews v. Eldridge*, 424 U.S. 319 (1976)).

~E~

Effective Date   As specified by the Constitution, the date when a law takes effect; the date is usually January 1 of the following year, unless the bill is an urgency measure or specifies another date.

Emergency Decision Making   Action first, review later; emergency rules may be promulgated under the Administrative Procedure Act without a hearing and will continue to be effective for a limited time until a rule-making hearing can be held.

Estoppel   An equitable doctrine that courts may or may not apply in a given situation. Agencies are not necessarily bound by what they have informally done or said in the past. When agencies seek to change their policy, developed through adjudication, they must give reasons for the change. Sanctions are not required to be consistent from case to case, so long as the sanctions remain within the statutory delegation and are not disproportionate.

Evaluation of Evidence   Agencies are viewed as experts in their particular areas; courts recognize that agencies have the expertise to interpret the evidence that generalist courts do not have, so reviewing courts are deferential to agency regarding evaluation of evidence. Evidence may be matters within the experience of ordinary individuals, or it may involve highly technical matters. Agencies must provide adequate evidentiary findings to support their choices; they may never use their expertise to add facts to a formal adjudication record after it has been closed.

Executive Session   A committee meeting restricted to committee members and invited guests.

Exempt From Review by the Office of Administrative Law   A statutory provision exempting a state agency from the Cal.-APA California Administrative Procedure Act requirement to submit proposed regulations and their supporting rule-making file to the Office of Administrative Law for review. Other APA requirements apply.

Exempt From the Administrative Procedure Act   A statutory provision exempting a state agency or its regulations from compliance with requirements in the Administrative Procedure Act.

Exhaustion   Parties seeking judicial review generally must demonstrate that they exhausted all the possible administrative opportunities for redress within the agency.

Ex Parte Contact with Administrative Judge   Evidence received without notice to the other side is received ex parte and cannot be used in a closed record decisional process. Ex parte contact may disqualify the judge based on bias, or it can end a case. The other, noncontacting side does not know what facts it needs to rebut. In an adjudication, the APA requires agencies to base their decisions on the evidence in the record, not on evidence received ex parte (Lat.: one-sided).

Explanation   Agencies must explain their use of evidence. In formal adjudications, the explanation is in the form of findings; in rule making, the explanation is the basis and purpose statement (if required by the APA); in a due process hearing, findings may be required (but not the formal type of findings required in the adjudication process). If agencies reject compelling evidence, courts may require agency decision makers to explain why the evidence was rejected.

~F~

Fact A piece of information. When reviewing courts characterize facts as general or common knowledge, they likely will substitute their judgment for that of the agency. When facts are technical or scientific, courts are more likely to defer to agency interpretation of what the facts mean.

Federal Register Daily government publication with notices of agencies' proposed rules and the final versions of rules/regulations for future enactment.

Fiscal Note The analysis of the financial impact of a proposed rule or rule change.

Fiscal Year A 12-month period during which a budget is in effect. The federal fiscal year begins October 1 and ends September 30 of the following year.

Finality Under the terms of most APAs, only final agency action is reviewable. Final agency action occurs when a rule is promulgated or an adjudication order is issued and served by the agency.

Findings Elements in the formal adjudication. Substantial evidence must exist to support the final determination and explain the particular elements that need to be proved. Insufficient findings can be a basis for remand to the agency. Where agencies announce a change in policy by formal adjudication, an explanation may be required; where strong evidence is rejected, there may be a requirement to explain the rejection. In due process hearings, findings may be required (but not the complete type of findings required in a formal adjudication). An adjudicatory decision must be accompanied by findings of fact and conclusions of law; in informal adjudication, some findings may be required to establish a basis for judicial review. Findings are needed to demonstrate that the agency has jurisdiction over a matter. Findings must be based on considerations as they existed at the time of decision making; they show that the decision maker took into account all of the factors in the statute. Demeanor credibility findings might need to be based on objective criteria. Where multiple allegations are in the notice of hearing, findings show which particular allegations were proved.

Follow Own Rules Agencies must follow their own rules to make valid decisions—a fundamental requirement of administrative law.

Full and Fair Hearing Requirement The record of an adversarial proceeding must be adequate for the bench officer to make findings on all statutorily and legally required elements.

~G~

General Factors Factors influencing courts in judicial review. Substantial evidence, proper findings, degree of interference with agency functions, the value of uniformity of agency decisions; judicial reluctance to interfere until fact-gathering ends and the agency has exercised the full extent of its discretion.

Grandfather Clause A new law's exemption from compliance for existing entities (sometimes called grandparenting).

Graymail A litigation tactic in which a government employee defendant claims that classified documents are essential to a successful defense; the government can be counted on to deny permission for use of these documents in trial. The defense asserts it cannot get a fair trial without them and demands dismissal of all charges.

~H~

Habeas Corpus   A writ, issued by a court on request, for a government authority to bring a prisoner to court and justify why the prisoner should continue to be detained (Lat.: you have the body).

Hearing   An adversarial proceeding in which an administrative bench officer takes evidence and arguments, then rules on administrative issues; a committee meeting to gather information on a specific subject or discuss acting on it.

Hearsay   A statement made outside of court, which is offered in court to prove the truth of the contents of that statement. It is considered unreliable because it is not subject to being tested through cross-examination, one of the crown jewels of American jurisprudence. Hearsay evidence is generally admissible in administrative proceedings, but it generally cannot be used as the sole basis for an agency decision (the administrative hearsay rule, the residuum rule). Numerous exceptions exist that either qualify out-of-court statements as not hearsay or allow admission of the statement despite the fact that it is hearsay; these apply in administrative proceedings as well as traditional civil court. For example, some documents can be shown to be sufficiently reliable for admission into the record without cross examination of all the people involved in producing them, but where cross-examination is not used, the opposing party should have an opportunity to submit rebuttal evidence.

Hijack   Deleting the contents of a bill and inserting all new provisions; may occur even without the author's permission.

~I~

Initiative   Lawmaking that requires a direct popular vote (not a vote of the legislature) for a measure to become law.

Injunction, Stay   Parties seeking judicial review of agency action sometimes seek a delay (stay) of the agency action pending completion of judicial review. A stay is not usually automatic; it must be requested.

Interpretation of Statutory Language   Courts are usually deferential to agency interpretation of its own statutes, justified by its specialized expertise. The vaguer the language of the enabling statute, the more interpretative discretion accorded to the agency.

Interpretative Rules   Agencies develop nonbinding rules as a guide to how the agency will exercise its authority; these can be memoranda, handbooks, or slide presentations. Agencies can change their interpretive rules at any time; there is no notice and comment requirement.

Introductory Statement (California)   Data explaining what action is being taken that precedes every rule submitted to the Office of Administrative Hearings for publication.

Investigation, Agency Action   Investigation generally precedes rule-making hearings; follows promulgation of legislative rules; and determines whether rule violations have occurred that trigger notice of formal adjudication.

~J~

Judicial Review   The process by which courts examine agency actions to determine consistency with the Constitution. The big issues in rule making include the adequacy of notice, whether the rule is within the statutory delegation of authority given to the agency, whether the "basis and purpose" statement is adequate (if one is required), and whether the minimal procedural steps were followed.

<h2 style="text-align:center">~L~</h2>

Legislative Facts vs. Adjudicative Facts Legislative facts are broad, requiring opinion or judgment to identify; adjudicative facts are specific data about specific situations. This distinction occurs in judicial review of agency decision making: reversible error is more likely when adjudicative facts, not legislative facts, are excluded; this focuses on the importance of data and information to due process in agency determinations.

Limitation Period A period after which judicial review may be obtained; a common time limit in APAs is 60 days after the agency makes a final decision. Counsel must check the rules of each agency to be sure.

<h2 style="text-align:center">~M~</h2>

Mental Processes of Decider In formal adjudication, the decider must use a personal, mental process to apply the law to the facts and issues. The agency decider designated in the statute must make a final decision for the agency.

Mitigation Reducing a consequence so it is less severe. In formal adjudication, the agency's action may impose a sanction on the offender, which the administrative bench officer can reduce; request for or order of mitigation should include an explanation of how the reduction in penalty achieves the goals of the statute.

Motion A formal request for action; a request to a court or tribunal.

Motion to Reconsider A request to reverse an action already taken.

<h2 style="text-align:center">~N~</h2>

Non-Acquiescence An agency's disagreement with and refusal to follow judicial precedent in cases before the agency to which the precedent applies. The practical impact is that similarly situated individuals may be treated differently depending on the circuit in which they live (primarily occurs in the federal system).

Notice Before an agency promulgates a rule, notice and an informal hearing process may be required. The language in the notice can later be used to test whether the final rule is within the terms in the notice; if the notice and the final rule diverge too greatly, the final rule may be opposed for failure to follow statutory procedures. Notice of formal adjudication requires informing the party of the charges.

Notice and Opportunity to Respond Minimum due process requirements; opportunity to respond does not require oral hearings (a response in writing alone may be adequate). Minimal due process procedures do not apply where statutes apply greater obligations or eliminate all due process obligations.

<h2 style="text-align:center">~O~</h2>

OAH Office of Administrative Hearings.

Objection Letter Written correspondence from the public objecting to a rule and requesting review.

Occupational Licensing Agency Any board, commission, committee, or other agency established for the primary purpose of regulating the entry of people into, and/

or the conduct of people within, a particular profession, occupation, or field of endeavor, and which is authorized to issue and revoke licenses.

Office of Administrative Law, OAL (California)   The independent executive branch agency responsible for reviewing state agency rule making and regulations for compliance with the procedures and standards of the Cal.-APA.

Official Notice   A way to add evidence to the record without introducing the actual evidence; similar to judicial notice but covering more types of evidence. Evidence is properly officially noticed if it is readily verifiable. Legislative facts are more likely to be officially noticed; this is less likely for adjudicative facts. The APA mandates an opportunity to rebut officially noticed evidence. Adding facts to the record is not the same as interpreting facts in the record; adding facts requires advance notice to the other side and permission from the hearing officer; interpretation of facts in the record does not require advance notice.

Order   The result of formal adjudication, direction from the bench regarding taking action or refraining from taking action.

Organic Statute, Enabling Statute   The legislation that authorizes an agency to act; judicial review of agency decisions involves examination of the governing APA and the organic (enabling) statute. The organic statute sets out the factors the agency must consider in reaching its decisions and may affect operation of the APA.

~P~

Paper or Oral   Due process requirements do not mandate oral hearings; adjudication may be limited to an exchange of paper. Most APAs give agencies discretion in this regard.

Personal Decision   The agency head must make all final determinations. Issues arise regarding how much preliminary assistance can be provided to or accepted by the agency head. The most important requirement regarding personal decision making involves adversarial adjudications; the agency head must not rubberstamp staff decisions. Outside advisory groups may assist the decision maker so long as the record is protected, the final decision is personal with the decision maker, and the decision is based solely on statutory factors.

Petition for Reconsideration   An aspect of an agency's exhaustion of remedies defense. Agencies may oppose requests for judicial review by arguing that parties should seek reconsideration by the agency before seeking judicial review. However, most APAs do not require a request for reconsideration after an agency issues its final decision.

Petition for Rule Making   Some APAs provide that individuals can ask an agency to develop regulations, sometimes because no rules exist at the time or because an amendment to existing rules is needed. Agencies have discretion to deny the petition.

Power to Remand or Reverse   The APA or enabling statute empowers a court to act after finding agency error; courts may have the power to remand, to enter a new decision, or to overturn the agency action.

Prehearing Conference   Usually telephonic, this call is scheduled before complicated or lengthy formal adjudication tribunals. Some agencies have created procedures for these conferences; the result of the conference is usually agreements regarding scheduling, handling evidence, and other issues.

Presumptions   Ideas believed to be true, including the honesty and integrity of agency decision makers and that agencies follow their own rules and procedures. Courts rely on presumptions during judicial review; the party challenging the agency action has the burden of overcoming the presumptions that support the agency.

Privilege of the Floor   Permission from the presiding officer of a government body for a person to view the proceedings from the floor of the chamber, rather than from the gallery; members request this courtesy for constituents and guests.

Procedure   Administrative system of rules that govern the processes of an agency, focused on efficiency, consistency, and accountability. A prescribed course of action; written rules of procedure, including administrative law, often codified in the federal or state APA.

Promulgation, Nonpromulgation, and Rescission (of a rule or regulation)   There are three types of rule making: promulgation of rules following the statutory requirements (most common); rescission of rules, which generally follows the same procedures as promulgation; beginning of rule-making and then deciding not to promulgate a final rule, which does not require the agency to follow a particular procedure.

Property Interests, Liberty Interests   The type of due process hearing required depends on whether a property interest (for example, the government discharges an employee, repossesses property, or proposes to terminate benefits, which trigger greater procedural protection) or a liberty or reputational interest (which triggers less procedural protection) is involved. The due process right that is granted is procedural (a hearing), rather than substantive.

Prosecutorial Discretion   Agencies have broad flexibility regarding whether or not to prosecute.

Public Participation   The process by which agencies consult with interested or affected individuals, organizations, and government entities during decision making. Public participation in decision-making hearings varies with the type of decision: the general public has a right to comment on legislative rule making; in formal adjudication, public involvement is discretionary (only the parties have a right to participate in an adjudication hearing); in informal adjudication, rights of participation vary greatly based on the terms of the statute involved and the procedural rules promulgated by the agency. Parties usually means individuals with participation rights; persons means members of the public; intervenor means individuals who may participate at the agency's discretion.

~Q~

Quasi-Legislative   Action of administrative agencies or their officers to make law, usually through rule making.

Questions on Review   Judicial review of agency decisions are generally not focused on whether the agency decision was right; the decision is split into various elements, and the proper scope of review is applied to each. Questions of fact are reviewed under the deferential substantial evidence test; the court can substitute its judgment for that of the agency on questions of law. Mixed questions of fact and law are broken down, with various elements allocated for decision primarily to the court or to the agency. Each element of the decision must be separately identified and discussed in light of the scope of review applied to that element.

Quorum   The minimum number of individuals needed to begin conducting official business of a government body.

~R~

Rebuttal Evidence   Evidence offered into the record to challenge evidence in the record; used where cross-examination is not available. Denial of the right to rebut may be prejudicial error in some administrative hearings.

Recess   A pause that halts a proceeding for a time but is not an adjournment.

Reconsideration   A motion that, if successful (the motion has carried), allows a measure that failed or passed to be reheard.

Record   The administrative file, including requests for determination, documents submitted regarding the request for determination, protests, submissions to the agency, documents expressing agency action, any information that is considered by the agency in making its decisions, documents required to be prepared by the statute, and final agency determination; some state APAs include staff communications with the decision maker. In formal adjudication, the record is the proceedings of the hearing, including prehearing conference agreements, official notice, and the decision by the bench officer. Once closed, the record is the exclusive source for fact-finding at the agency level and the sole source for application of the substantial evidence test in judicial review. The record may include only data that was available at the time the decision was made; judicial review may occur months or years later; post hoc rationalization based on posthearing information cannot be used.

Regulation(s)   Detailed rules that implement legislation; focused on requirements of what, how, by whom, where, and when. Agency rule, which has the force of law, to carry out a legislative or administrative mandate. Under the APA, must meet certain standards for adoption.

Regulatory Analysis   Various studies needed before an agency adopts a regulation; includes impact on small business and record-keeping.

Regulatory Impact Analysis   A study about a proposed regulation, including a statement of need for the regulation; assessment of alternative regulatory approaches; benefit-cost analysis (see above); and, sometimes, cost-effectiveness analyses.

Repeal   To delete the entire text of a rule; the rule's number, name, and history sometimes remain in the code for reference purposes.

Residuum Rule, Administrative Hearsay Rule   Agency administrative decisions may not be based entirely on hearsay evidence; instead, a residuum of non-hearsay evidence must exist and support the decision.

Res Judicata   Doctrine barring claims that have been litigated or that could have been litigated from being relitigated (Lat.: A thing already judged).

Resolution   An opinion of the legislature that does not have the force of law and that does not require the governor's signature.

Right to Representation   Parties to formal administrative adjudication have a right to be represented by private counsel; none will be appointed.

Ripeness   Requirement to trigger judicial review of agency action; identifies the concreteness of the issue and whether a court can resolve the matter. The agency action must be ripe to be granted judicial review; final agency action meets the ripeness test.

Role of Judicial Review of Agency Action   Judicial review is the final procedural step in the administrative law process.

Rule   Agency regulation, standard, or statement of general applicability that implements or interprets a legislative enactment; an agency regulation describing the procedure or practice requirements of that agency. Standards governing operations.

Rule Making   The FAPA (and some state APAs) require a basis-and-purpose statement for every proposed regulation. In federal court review, this shows that the agency considered other statements of the regulation.

Rule-Making Agency   An agency with statutory authority to adopt regulations.

Rule-Making Authority   Enabling statute that empowers an agency to adopt regulations.

Rule-Making Coordinator   Individual identified by an agency to oversee the agency's process for adopting regulations.

~S~

Sanction   Penalty for disobeying a rule; if an agency finds a violation, it can impose a penalty (sanction) as allowed in the enabling statute. Also means permission or approval.

Scope of Review   Courts use various tests to analyze agency decisions, including "arbitrary and capricious" or "clear error of judgment" tests. Courts analyze agency explanations of rejection of contrary evidence, allowing agencies to choose any reasonable option, or approving agency decisions that are reasonable but not necessarily right. Courts defer to reasonable agency interpretations unless the enabling statute is clear and the agency failed to follow its clear terms; if the statute's wording is ambiguous, the agency interpretation (and its choice of sanctions) are given great deference. Courts will not substitute their judgment for that of the agency if the agency is reasonable on the facts, but courts can substitute their judgment on the law.

Separation of Agency Functions   Combining investigatory and adjudicatory responsibility is not absolutely prohibited (multiple agency functions may be involved in a file, including investigation, advocating, judging, deciding, and settlement attempts). Combining advocacy and deciding gets closest to a disqualifying bias; specific instances, examples, or effects of the alleged bias are required for disqualification.

Settlement   Negotiated resolution; most agency disputes settle before the matter goes to formal adjudication.

Short Committee   The total of those in attendance is less than a quorum.

Site Visit   A trip to a relevant location; a substitute for a portion of a formal or informal hearing process. Where a full hearing record is required, the results of the visit must be preserved in the record in some form.

Specificity and Substantial Prejudice Regarding Bias   The burden of proof is on the appellant to show specific bias, resulting in specific and substantial prejudice (general allegations or a generally unfriendly atmosphere are insufficient). A general allegation of bias is inadequate to show agency error.

Spot Bill   A bill that amends a code section in a nonsubstantive way.

Staff Opinion, Staff Recommendation   Reasoned position of counsel regarding whether the government body should approve or object to a rule.

Standing   The standing requirement is a prequalification for judicial review of agency action. The most common requirement is "injury in fact." When organizations seek standing, they must show that either the organization itself has actually been injured or one of its members has been injured and the organization represents that member.

State Action   Any action taken by a government. Due process requirements apply only to state action.

Statutes   Compilation of all enacted bills.

Stop the Clock   To continue business after time has expired.

Summary Digest   Brief summaries of legislation passed in the legislative session, listed in the order they were signed into law.

Sunset Date   A date included in a measure after which it automatically becomes ineffective.

Sunset Provision   An expiration date included in a proposal.

Sunshine Law   Statute designed to open government records to public inspection.

~T~

Telephone Hearing   Administrative tribunal that proceeds exclusively by telephone, presided over by an administrative hearing officer, with no in-person element; documentary evidence is distributed in advance. Although telephone hearings prevent personal confrontation, this does not offend due process.

Testing   Scientific process; testing may substitute for a hearing regarding safety.

Thirty-Day Provision, 30-Day Provision   The 30-day waiting period following a bill's introduction, before it may be heard or acted on by some legislatures.

Timing of Hearing   Constitutional due process considerations do not require that due process hearings take place before the government acts; hearings may occur before or after the action.

Types of Rules   Formal rule making; usually requires hearings with notice. Notice-and-comment rule making (informal rule making); opportunity to comment sometimes includes oral hearing (no statutory requirement for a closed record). Interpretative rule making; issuance of rules, often in the form of a handbook, that explain the agency's working interpretation of the statute (interpretative rules are not binding on courts).

~U~

Underground Regulation (California)   Agency regulations that should have been but were not adopted through proper procedures under the Cal.-APA; they are invalid.

Unreviewability (by a court)   When an agency has been granted discretion to act and a reviewing court cannot find in the statute granting this discretion any provisions for appeal to a court for judicial review, the court lacks jurisdiction (power) to review the agency action. A statute may expressly preclude judicial review, or preclusion can be implicit.

Index